# The Stag Cook Book
## Written for Men by Men

**Alexandre Dumas**

**The Stag Cook Book: Written for Men by Men**

ISBN: 979-8-88830-289-7

Dedicated To—

THAT GREAT HOST
OF BACHELORS AND BENEDICTS ALIKE
who have at one time or another tried to "cook something"; and who, in the attempt, have weakened under a fire of feminine raillery and sarcasm, only to spoil what, under more favorable circumstances, would have proved a chef-d'œuvre.

# CONTENTS

*"They may live without houses and live without books,"*
*So the saying has gone through the ages,*
*"But a civilized man cannot live without cooks—"*
*It's a libel, as proved by these pages!*
*For when left by himself in a small kitchenette,*
*With a saucepan, a spoon and a kettle,*
*A man can make things that you'll never forget—*
*That will put any cook on her mettle.*

*Where camp fires glow through the still of the night,*
*Where grills are electric and shiny,*
*Where kitchens are huge, done in tiling of white,*
*Where stoves are exceedingly tiny,*
*Where people are hungry—no matter the place—*
*A man can produce in a minute*
*A dish to bring smiles to each skeptical face,*
*With art—and real food value—in it!*

*At range and at oven, at (whisper it!) still,*
*A man is undoubtedly master;*
*His cooking is done with an air and a skill,*
*He's sure as a woman—and faster!*
*He may break the dishes and clutter the floor,*
*And if he is praised—he deserves it—*
*He may flaunt his prowess until he's a bore. . . .*
*But, Boy, what he serves—when he serves it!*

# INTRODUCTION

## By Robert H. Davis

Cooking is a gift, not an art. Eating is an art, not a gift. In combination a grace is developed. No great culinary triumph was ever perfected by accident.

Charles Lamb's essay on roast pig was responsible for a tidal wave of burnt pork that swept over England in the nineteenth century. Mr. Lamb led a hungry empire to the belief that only through an act of incendiarism could a suckling porker be converted into a delicacy; whereas, as a matter of fact, the perfection of roast pork, golden-brown and unseared by fire, were possible only in the oven.

Lucullus, the good Roman gourmet, had his meals cooked in a mint. He required that his masterpieces be served on gold and silver and crystal, and spread on a table of lapis lazuli. The sauces compiled for him were worth more than the food upon which they were poured. He was the high priest of extravagance and luxury. A single meal stood him a fortune. He had more regard for the cost than for the cooking. It is said that his death was hastened by dyspepsia.

In the early seventies a French nobleman, living in the neighborhood of Barbizon, was found seated at the table with his face in a plate of soup. Because of the fact that a butcher knife had been inserted via the back between his fourth and fifth rib on the left side, he was quite dead. Clues led nowhere. It became one of the mysteries.

Long afterward an old man tottered into the office of the Prefect and announced that he wished to make a confession.

"Proceed," said the official.

"'Twas I," responded the ancient, "who delivered the death stroke to the Duke de la —— thirty-five years ago."

"What inspired you to make this confession?"

"Pride."

"I do not comprehend. The details, if you please."

"By profession I was a chef," said the self-accused. "The Duke, at a fabulous price, enticed me into his service. His first request was that I make for him a perfect consomme. Voilà! For three days I prepared this perfection. With my own hand I placed before him the soup tureen. With my own hand I ladled it out. He inhaled its divine essence; and then, Your Honor, he reached for the salt. Mon Dieu! I destroy him!"

The Prefect embraced the artist and took him out to lunch. Thus art was vindicated and the incident closed. In the chemistry of cooking, "enough is too much."

The immortals who have contributed recipes to this volume were born with a silver spoon not in their mouths, but in their hands. The cap and apron, not the cap and bells, is the garb in which they perform. Secrets handed down through generations are thrown with a wanton hand on the pages that comprise this volume. Sauces from the south, chowders from New England, barbecued masterpieces from the west, grilled classics from field and stream, ragouts, stews, desserts, dressings are hung within reach of all, like garlic clusters from the rafters of opportunity. Reach up and help yourself.

Be not disturbed by occasional jocund phrases in this symposium. Behind them is probably concealed a savory or a flavor. A long paragraph may conclude with full particulars concerning the architecture of a gastronomic dream. Turn the pages slowly lest you be overwhelmed by the richness of the menu.

The late King Edward, upon bidding the later Carlos of Portugal God-speed back to his native shores, inquired: "By what were you most impressed during your visit to the British Isles?"

"Roast beef," said Carlos, expanding in ecstasy.

"And what else?" inquired Edward.

"Well," said Carlos, "the boiled beef wasn't so damned bad."

It is one thing to cook food, and another to consume it. This inspired tome is the product of cooks who are not afraid to take their own medicine. The names of many of the dishes catalogued herein lies on the tongues of the mob, but the delicacies themselves do not. This book brings within the reach of all opportunities that up to now have been denied them. Given a first class stove, a few simple ingredients and a copy of this book, hunger can be abolished wherever English is read.

Rossini, the musician, also a chef, after writing the score of The Barber of Seville, was informed by the director that a prelude was required immediately. Rossini repaired to his kitchen, cooked himself a perfect dinner, consumed it alone, and went to bed where in a reclining position with score sheets all about him, he wrote a brilliant introduction to his brilliant opera. Suddenly a gust of wind entered unbidden at the window and scattered the precious sheets about the room. Several disappeared through the lattice. Rossini, heavy with the consequences of his culinary genius, re-wrote a fresher and better prelude, tucked it under his corpulent person and rolled over for a final nap, after which he hastened to the opera house with his masterpiece. His best work was done on a full stomach.

Brillat-Savarin, author of "Gastronomy as a Fine Art," rather whimsically names "Gasteria" the tenth and fairest of the Muses. The writers of this book name her as the first.

R. H. D.

# THE STAG COOK BOOK

"This dish of meat is too good for
any but anglers, or very honest men."

Izaak Walton

1

# I

## Meredith Nicholson

## WABASH VALLEY STEAK

No man can be a hero in his own kitchen. No man with the slightest regard for domestic peace will ever permit his wife to see him cook without having outsiders present. The psychology of this is obvious. Impatient though a woman may be of her husband's attempts to show that he is a real sport and skilled in all the arts of social entertaining, before guests she is likely to manifest a modest degree of pride in his performances. Or even if slightly contemptuous she is moved to assume a chaffing attitude that adds to the general good feeling. I beg not to be confused with the type of bachelor club man who is a perfect wizard with the chafing dish. I have always viewed those birds with suspicion. Their tricks are few and easy of accomplishment—stunts with mushrooms, or chicken à la king done nonchalantly in a dinner coat. I sing my fiercest hymn of hate of those persons.

My own method is to assume full charge of an orderly kitchen, removing coat and waistcoat, donning an apron and attacking the job without apology or simper or the silly pretense that I'm not sure of the result. Not sure! Except in the case of colored women cooks, who trust to inspiration and achieve miracles without, seemingly, knowing how they do 'em—except, I say, in such instances, cookery is an exact science. If you follow a good rule and know how to regulate the range and have a true eye and acute nose, failure is obliterated from the lexicon.

And now for my scenario, which I stole from a lady, who in turn stole it, I dare say, from some cook book. I might pretend that I invented it, but I didn't. All I claim is that it offers an Olympian feast—particularly if you can accompany it with hot biscuits, which I admit are beyond my powers.

### The Recipe

Take a round steak cut two inches thick; and beat a cup of flour into it. Heat a large skillet till it is piping hot with lard covering

2

the bottom about one inch. Put in the steak, cover immediately, and allow it to cook about five minutes, turning once.

Then cover it with a sauce composed in this wise:

*Four large tomatoes*
*Four onions*
*Four green mango peppers*
*Four ripe pimentoes*

Put through a grinder or better still chop thoroughly with a chopper in a wooden bowl. Don't skimp on this labor; the chopping must be done conscientiously. Season with salt and pour over the steak; cook slowly for two hours. When done turn into a large platter and serve piping hot.

# II

## Rex Beach

# ONION CLAM CHOWDER

To each 10 oz. can of Pioneer Brand Minced Clams use 1 pound of sliced Spanish or white onion.

For a good sized chowder take six large onions (white), and cut in lengths one inch long. Pour the juice from the clams into saucepan, add onions and a little water and boil thoroughly until onions are well cooked and soft. Then add clams which have been taken out of the can and put into a dish, and stew five minutes before onions are done. Next place in a stew pan about a pint of cream or half cream and half milk and let come to a boil. After the clams have been in with the onions for about three minutes pour on the hot milk and season to taste with salt and pepper. If serving in a soup plate, a little chopped parsley adds to the attractiveness of the dish. Then EAT it.

(You can substitute for fresh milk or cream—Carnation Canned Milk diluted—⅔ milk to ⅓ water. The soup should be thick and not too watery. This can be regulated by amount of milk added.)

# III

## Hudson Maxim

## SPAGHETTI

Take one package of vermicelli or spaghetti, and put it into a saucepan, crushing it in the hand, then put in hot water, and salt a little more than will suit the taste, and boil for an hour.

While the vermicelli or spaghetti is cooking, take a quart of milk and heat three-quarters—or 24 ounces—of it until it boils. Then stir into the eight ounces of cold milk a level cupful of flour, or two tablespoonfuls of flour, pretty well heaped, and then stir the thickened milk into the boiling milk and cook slowly for ten minutes.

Then add three-quarters of a pound of good, ripe, old American cheese, and about half a pound of butter. Then drain the water off the vermicelli or spaghetti and put in from one and one half pints to a quart of canned tomatoes. Heat the vermicelli or spaghetti to the boiling point; and while the mixture of cheese, butter, milk and flour is still hot, stir the two together, then keep hot and serve hot. Do not boil any more, because further boiling would tend to cause the tomatoes to coagulate the milk in the mixture. I prefer to use a mixture of spaghetti and vermicelli instead of all spaghetti or all vermicelli.

5

# IV

## Warren G. Harding

## WAFFLES

2 eggs
2 tablespoons sugar
2 tablespoons butter
1 teaspoon salt
1 pint milk
flour to make thin batter
2 large teaspoons of baking powder

Beat yolks of eggs, add sugar and salt, melt butter, add milk and flour; last just before ready to bake add beaten whites of eggs and baking powder.

Bake on hot waffle iron.

*Editor's Note*:—There is a great deal of argument about the proper dressing for waffles. Various gravies are used by one school of waffle eaters; while honey, maple syrup, and various specially flavored sugar powders are preferred by another.

President Harding is a staunch upholder of the gravy school and likes his in the form of creamed chipped beef.

# V

## Ellis Parker Butler

## BOUILLABAISSE JOE TILDEN

In a soup kettle put four tablespoonsful of genuine olive oil. When hot enough fry in it two large onions, sliced, and two cloves of garlic chopped. Cut two pounds of any sort of firm white-textured fish into small pieces and put in the kettle, just covering the mixture with warm water.

Now have the Eighteenth Amendment repealed and add to the mixture one cup of White Wine, the juice of half a lemon, two large tomatoes (peeled and cut up), pepper, salt and one or two bay leaves.

Cook this briskly for twelve minutes, by which time the liquor should be one third evaporated. Now add a tablespoonful of chopped parsley. Joe Tilden added a pinch of saffron, but I don't care for it. Cook two minutes longer and serve ladled on slices of French bread.

Editor's Note:—Moquin's have made a luncheon specialty of Bouillabaisse for many years. They add lobster and eel. Here is a wonderful dish to experiment with—great fun and delicious results if you try it once or twice. It's a habit-forming dish, so beware!

# VI

## Jules J. Jusserand

### (Ambassador to the United States from France)

### RADISH SALAD

The French ambassador presents his compliments and begs to state that he does not believe that any dish, or food, is more palatable than a salad of radishes, the radishes to be cut in very thin slices and to be seasoned with the usual salad dressing.

Editor's Note:—This salad will be at its best if the foundation, upon which the thin slices of radish are placed, is made of small crisp leaves of romaine. The usual dressing—french, of course—is prepared in this way:

To one tablespoonful of lemon or vinegar add three tablespoonsful of the best olive oil, a dash of black pepper, and a half teaspoonful of salt. Beat well with a silver fork, and add enough paprika to give it a ruddy color, and a rich flavor. If the salad dish is rubbed with garlic it will do no great harm to the mixture!

# VII

## Bruce Barton

## RICE PUDDING

I am president of the S. R. R. R. P.—the Society for Restoration of Raisins to Rice Pudding.

I have made a list of New York hotels and clubs and rated them according to the number of raisins they put in a portion of rice pudding as follows:

Class D—no raisins
Class C—1 raisin
Class B—3 or more raisins
Class A—plenty of raisins

To my mind, rice pudding without raisins is like Hamlet without the eggs.

1 cup rice
4 cups milk
3 eggs
½ cup sugar
1 teaspoonful salt
1 package seedless raisins
1 teaspoon of vanilla

Bake one hour in a hot oven. Set the pan inside of another containing hot water.

Serve with whipped cream and garnish with Dromedary dates.

*Editor's Note:*—Cook the rice twenty-three minutes.

# VIII

## Richard Bennett

## LIEDERKRANZ Á LA HOOSIER

Run around and find a real nice Liederkranz cheese and treat it as follows to get a serving for four people:

Mix the cheese with about a quarter of a pound of butter and work into a fine paste, adding salt, pepper, French mustard, paprika and Worcestershire sauce as you go along. Just add them to taste.

When the paste is smooth put in one finely chopped small green pepper; one small onion, or chives.

Mix well!

And serve on rye bread—spread thick. To be thoroughly technical, I suppose I should have said: spread to taste!

*Editor's Note:*—You can have a wonderful time and make quite a reputation for yourself by inventing cheese combinations. Ordinary cream cheese makes a splendid base for original mixtures. Try combinations of finely minced pimento, celery, olives, chives and peppers (green and red). And anything else that promises well.

# IX

## Walt Louderback

## CORN CHOWDER

*I believe my favorite recipe is Corn Chowder.*
The appetite for this dish must be approached from the windy side of a promontory in early spring with a sixty pound pack between the shoulder blades, aforementioned pack to contain for a couple of congenial souls a pound of bacon, a pound of dry onions, two cans of corn and one large tin of condensed milk.

Cut the bacon up into small half inch squares and start it frying. Simultaneously slice the onions and give them the heat. If, after the aroma from these two begins to permeate the air, you feel like risking their falling into the fire, start boiling the corn and milk. Before the onions are too thoroughly cooked stir them into the bacon, at which time the battle for the supremacy of the appetizing odors is occupying most of your attention.

Now throw the bacon and onions into the corn pot and wait as long as you are able so that the ingredients become thoroughly familiar with one another.

Write me as soon as you get home if you don't remember that day until you are an old man.

To make this sound extremely professional I suppose I should add, "Season to taste," but do not mind if a few ashes get mixed in by mistake.

# X

## Captain Robert A. Bartlett, U.S.A.

### COD FISH

Here is my favorite dish. Viz.:—Fresh Labrador Codfish caught during the Caplin school. The fish is at this time in splendid condition.

Here is the recipe:

Place a small bake pot upon a wood fire; then take a few strips of fat pork, cut up into small pieces and put into the bake pot. When the pork fat has melted you cut the fish into several small pieces and place in the pot. In about twenty minutes the fish is cooked. The fish must be eaten from the pot with a wooden spoon.

# XI

## George F. Worts

## SWEET POTATO PONE

There are two sure ways of identifying a true southerner. One of them is to play "Dixie." Unlike your northerner, or counterfeit southerner who springs to his feet and looks exalted and proud when the band strikes up that swinging anthem, your true, or southern southerner rarely springs. Generally he just sets and waggles one boot, and looks happy or sentimental, according to his nature. That is one way of detecting your true southerner. The second and surer way is to announce in a tremulous voice: "Gemmen, dat potato pone am done set."

The sweet potato pone is strictly a southern dish. It is served south of the Mason and Dixon line hot and smoking. You don't need much experience as a cook, although the old rule which also places "perfect" after "practice" of course holds good. Your ninth potato pone will be better than your third. Here is the how:

Grind up raw sweet potatoes in a meat chopper until you have one quart. Mix the grindings thoroughly in a bowl with molasses— enough molasses so the mass is soft and sticky, or spongy.

Mix in a heaping tablespoonful of lard.

Add a teaspoonful of allspice.

Put the mixture in a cake tin and place in a slow oven. Stir constantly until a rich brown hue is attained, then smooth over with a knife or spoon and allow to bake slowly until a mellow brown crust is formed.

Remove from oven, allow to cool slightly, cut in slices and serve. General Robert E. Lee would walk ten miles for a slice of it.

# XII

## Gelett Burgess

## PANDOWDY

In a quart pudding dish arrange alternate layers of sliced apples and bits of bread; place on each layer dots of butter, a little sugar, and a pinch each of ground cinnamon, cloves and allspice.

When the dish is filled, pour over it half a cupful each of molasses and water, mixed well; cover the top with bread crumbs.

Place the dish in a pan containing hot water, and bake for three-quarters of an hour, or until the apples are soft.

Serve hot, with cream or any light pudding sauce.

Raisins or chopped almonds are sometimes added.

# XIII

## William Allen White

## VEGETABLE SALAD

My idea of good food is a vegetable salad. Any kind of a vegetable salad is good; some are better than others. Here is a recipe for a French dressing on a lettuce salad which you should try on your meat grinder, or your potato masher, or your rolling pin or whatever kitchen utensil you can play.

Get a crisp head of lettuce, discard the outer green leaves, using the inner yellow and white. Wash it thoroughly, and after pulling it apart dry each leaf with a tea towel. Put it in a big bowl—a big mixing bowl, six inches deep anyway. Then set that to one side, and get about as much onion as the end of your first finger would make, if it was chopped off at the second joint. Mince that. Put it in the bottom of a bowl. Take a large tablespoon; put in salt and paprika to taste, and don't be afraid of making it salty, then add oil and vinegar, about three or four to one, mixing them in the spoon until it slops over into the onion, and then stir the salt and paprika and oil and vinegar down into the bowl of minced onion, taking a salad fork and jabbing it around in the mixture until the onion has been fairly well crushed and the onion flavor permeates the mixed oil and vinegar, and the salt and paprika have become for the moment a part of the mass. Don't let it stand a second, but pour it quickly into the bowl of dry lettuce, and then stir like the devil. Keep on stirring; stir some more, and serve as quickly as possible.

Cheese may be mashed into the onion before putting on the oil and vinegar and paprika and salt. If one wants to add tomatoes, wait until the last three jabs of the stirring fork into the lettuce, and then quarter the tomatoes and turn them in just before you turn the lettuce over the last two or three times. This is done so that the watery juice of the tomatoes won't get smeared over the oil on the lettuce leaves. If you stir the tomatoes in early, you get a runny, watery, gooey mess. Cucumbers may be added, and they should be stirred in rather earlier than the tomatoes in the business of mixing the lettuce leaves and the dressing. Green peppers may be added if they are cut into strings, but too much outside fixings spoils the salad for me. The tomatoes are about as far as one can go wisely.

15

# XIV

## Irvin S. Cobb

## HOG JOWL AND TURNIP GREENS

*Paducah Style*

For a person who has written so copiously about food and the pleasures of eating it, I probably know less of the art of preparing it than any living creature. I cannot give my favorite recipe because I have none; but I am glad to give the names of my two favorite dishes, to wit, as follows:

1st—Hog jowl and turnip greens—Paducah style
2nd—Another helping of the same.

*Editor's Note:*—Hog Jowl, Paducah Style, may be prepared like this:

Get the jowl. Some prefer it cooked and served with the bone; others remove the bone before serving. Boil it in well salted water for thirty minutes, then add the turnip greens and boil at least thirty minutes longer. Serve with plenty of butter for dressing; a dash of vinegar and a semi-colon of mustard are used by some folks who are hard to please.

Beet greens could be used but they are not considered au fait, and to use spinach is an absolute faux pas.

# XV

## Richard Walton Tully

## HAWAIIAN CROQUETTES Á LA "THE BIRD OF PARADISE"

It was about fifteen years ago that I first visited the Hawaiian Islands in search of material for my play, "The Bird of Paradise," and during the course of my sojourn I made many friends among the natives, often living weeks at a time with them in out-of-the-way villages. Although their food was radically different from ours in many of its contents and modes of making, it was always palatable, and often strikingly delicious. However, most of the native dishes contained ingredients which we cannot obtain here, but I did learn how to make what some of my friends have nick-named Hawaiian Croquettes à la "Bird of Paradise," the materials for which are easily procured. And it is a dish so wonderfully appetizing that I constantly prepare it for guests of epicurean tastes.

First grate the meat of half a cocoanut, and add to it a cup of (cow's) milk, mixing thoroughly, and straining through cloth. Melt two tablespoonsful of butter over a low flame, rubbing into it with the back of a spoon five tablespoonsful of flour, stirring until very smooth. Then add slowly the strained cocoanut and milk liquid, stirring constantly until very thick. Season meanwhile with one and a half teaspoonsful of salt; one of paprika, and one of grated onion. Finally add two cups of cold, boiled, shredded mullet, or any other firm white fish, and two cups of cold, boiled, chopped lobster, and after stirring allow to cool.

Shape into croquettes, or balls, allowing a rounded tablespoonful to each ball; roll in fine cracker crumbs; dip into an egg which has been slightly beaten and to which one-quarter of a cup of water has been added; again roll in cracker crumbs.

Have a deep pan of fat, hot enough to fry a piece of bread a golden brown while you count forty, and cook the croquettes therein for about a minute; then drain on paper, and serve with olives.

# XVI

## William Johnston

## OYSTERS PECHEUR

One keg of freshly dredged oysters put on the deck of the schooner not later than eight p. m.

One hundred pounds of ice put on top of the oysters.

Shell and eat at 5 a. m. on the way to the fishing grounds with salt to taste, and occasional draughts of hot coffee.

# XVII

## Dr. Charles M. Sheldon

## LIKES BREAD AND MILK

A recipe of my favorite dish is very simple—bread and milk with American cheese broken into it. I eat this dish once a day every day and find it wholesome and nourishing. It does not require any skillful putting together, simply a good appetite and a taste for that sort of provender. If there is an apple pie anywhere around to top it off with, I do not despise that.

I find as a rule that the simpler and more elementary the food, the better so far as the body is concerned. And take it the year around a bowl of milk with fresh bread and rich American cheese, finishing up with "good apple pie like mother used to make," is all the midday meal I need. I can work on that all the afternoon and feel better than if I had had a seven course dinner.

# XVIII

## James Montgomery Flagg

## "JAMES MONTGOMERY SUDS"

This is a dessert. When a Swedish cook is put on her mettle to suggest a dessert—something different—she stands a while in uffish thought, then breaks out into a smile of satisfaction and says "Snow Pudding"! It's Swede law. The Swedes must suggest Snow Pudding when asked for an original thought in the dessert line.

So this dessert of mine was a protest.

There is one very difficult ingredient—wine jelly! The jelly is easy enough, but where in Jell do you get the wine?

If you don't have wine jelly—it's all off—no use beginning. If you can get the wine then you put some cut-up oranges in wine jelly with an inch layer of beaten whites of eggs on top and lightly brown this. A loose custard is poured on each helping. It sounds rather punk and ladieshomejournalish but is a perfectly good dessert.

# XIX

## Roy L. McCardell

## "EGGS MUSHROOMETTE"

This is the queen of breakfast dishes and should be served, of course, with broiled ham, the king of breakfast dishes, hot buttered toast, and several cups of fresh-made, fragrant and just-strong-enough-to-bring-out-full-flavor, percolated coffee!

### Recipe

Peel and slice a half pound of fresh mushrooms and cook in butter in old-fashioned frying pan till nearly done. The pan is now good and hot. Moderate the heat and put in three fresh eggs and fry them very slowly, constantly basting top of eggs with the hot butter the mushrooms have been cooking in. Cook well, slowly and thoroughly till all the mushrooms that attach are nestling in the white of the eggs like plums in a pudding. Serve, when thoroughly cooked, with the broiled ham, fresh coffee, and hot buttered toast.

This dish, as here described, is for one person only—as it is too good to be shared with anybody else.

P. S.—Eggs should never be fried so quickly that the whites are cooked to isinglass. Cook them slowly, surely, thoroughly and baste with hot mushroom butter as directed, and you will have Eggs Mushroomette and have eaten a poem!

# XX

## Judge Ben B. Lindsey

## BRAN MUFFINS

Judge Lindsey's favorite recipe is one for Bran Muffins, as follows:

> 1 pint milk
> 1 egg
> ½ pound wheat flour
> ¾ pound bran flour
> 2 tablespoonsful molasses
> 2 ounces pecan meats (½s or ¼s)
> 2 ounces sugar
> 2 ounces butter
> ¼ ounce salt
> 2 ounces Sultana raisins
> 1 ounce baking powder

Sufficient for 18 muffins.
Bake 30 minutes in well-heated oven.

*Editor's Note:*—The addition of Pecan meats with the raisins produces a muffin that—well, the line might better have ended thus: produces a muffin!

# XXI

## Otis Skinner

## ARTICHOKES, MISTER ANTONIO

Force a small opening in the head of the artichoke by giving it a blow upon the table. Then, into the center pour a dessertspoonful of olive oil in which a little salt and pepper have been mixed. To this add a quarter of a clove of garlic.

Place the artichokes in such position that they may not be overturned. Surround them with cold water, and allow them to boil, covered and undisturbed, for half an hour.

This is an Italian method, and by following it one may understand why an artichoke need not taste as flat as boiled hay.

# XXII

## Dan Beard

## A BURGOO

Clean and dress the meat of a soft-shelled turtle, a painted turtle, a poker-dot turtle, or almost any other kind of turtle. Clean and dress a rabbit, a ruffled grouse, moose meat, elk meat, deer meat, sheep meat, in fact any sort of game. Cut your meat into pieces about the size of inch cubes. Save the bones, especially the marrow bones, to put in with the meat. Add some salt pork cut into cubes, if you have it.

If you have been thoughtful enough to supply your outfit with some ill-smelling, but palatable dry vegetables, they will add flavor to your burgoo, put all the material in a kettle, and fill the kettle half full of water. If you have beans and potatoes do not put them in with the meat because they will go to the bottom and scorch. While the stuff you have already put in the kettle is boiling, or simmering, peel your onions and quarter them, scrape your carrots and slice them, peel your potatoes, cut them up into pieces—about inch cubes. After your caldron has commenced to boil dump in the fresh vegetables, they will cool off the water and kill the boil. Do not let it come to a boil again, but put it over a slow fire and allow it to simmer. There should always be enough water to cover the vegetables. A can of tomatoes will add greatly to the flavor. Use no sweet vegetables like beets or sweet potatoes. Put the salt and pepper in just before you take it off the fire. When the burgoo is done, strain it into tin cups. The liquid out of an olive bottle adds greatly to the flavor if you pour it in while the stew is cooking. If you have such luxuries in camp as olives and lemons, a slice of lemon with an olive in each cup over which the liquid is poured makes a dish too good for any old king that ever lived.

The excellence of a burgoo depends upon two things, the materials you have of which to make it and the care you take in cooking it. No two burgoos are alike, and every one I ever tasted was mighty good. Civilized material such as can be purchased at the butcher shop and the vegetable store makes a good soup, but the "goo" isn't there. Consequently you cannot call it a burgoo.

# XXIII

## De Wolf Hopper

## RASPBERRY SHORTCAKE

RASPBERRY SHORTCAKE, with the assistance of a rich and kindly disposed cow, meaning lacteal fluid on same—that is my chief debauch!

### Recipe (for two people)

Sift a level teaspoonful of baking powder and a scant half teaspoonful of salt through a cupful of flour. See that the mixture is thorough. Take lard or butter (butter is best) and work it well into the flour until it crumbles under the fingers. Use plenty of finger work. Now add a very small quantity of milk and work into a dough that is easily rolled and flattened on a floured board. Roll out and cut in round cakes to fit cake tins. Have cakes about a half inch thick. Bake in a moderate oven until light golden in color. In serving have lots of berries—half of them—crushed. Split the shortcakes and butter them, if desired. Above all use thick, rich cream in generous doses. The dish is really best when the cakes are just from the oven—instead of cold.

The same goes for strawberry shortcake and makes the only real genuine old-fashioned shortcake.

# XXIV

## Chick Evans

## TOMATO SOUP

I have a fondness for tomato soup and steak without grizzles. Since almost any one can broil a steak I'll pass that up and tell you how to play cream of tomato right around the kitchen course in par.

You can take ripe tomatoes, cut them up, stew them and put them through a strainer. You can add a bit of soup stock and seasoning and all that, but the easy way is to take some of Mr. Campbell's tomato soup and add milk instead of water—only use more soup, per person, than the can label calls for.

Don't boil it—but when the soup is good and hot give it a bit of informal seasoning and then stir in a lot of stiff whipped cream. Keep back enough of the whipped cream to put a big spoonful of it in the center of each plate.

Use the can opener at the first tee and with luck you'll be on the dinner table in an easy three. Play out of the soup plate with a good sized spoon for a par four—and there you are!

You'll be able to whip the cream without detailed directions. The important thing is choosing the right egg beater or cream whipper or whatever you use. The next important thing in whipping cream is stance. You'll gradually acquire that, after you've spattered the front of your vest a time or two, and hooked a few long ones to the wall paper. I believe that there are some safety devices for whipping cream, but they take all the sport and excitement out of the thing.

# XXV

## Joshua A. Hatfield

## EGGPLANT SAUTÉ À L'ALEXANDER

*For About 12 People*

Take two large eggplants, have them peeled and cut into large flakes of about 1¼ inches in size, season with pepper and salt, pass through flour and fry in hot fat pan to brown color; chop finely and sauté to yellow color, six French shallots and two beans of garlic, and add to the eggplant. Keep stirring on moderate fire for about three minutes, serve in vegetable dish and spray with chopped parsley.

## POTATO STICKS ALEXANDER

Take six nice boiled potatoes, let them drain and pass through sieve, put in stewing pan on the fire, add four yolks of eggs, one spoonful of fresh butter, one spoonful of puff paste; one green pepper, one sweet pepper, two slices of boiled ham and parsley all finely chopped, and pepper and salt to taste.

Mix while on the fire for about five minutes, then let it cool down.

Of this dough roll sticks of ½ inch in diameter by 1½ inches long, pass through flour, beaten egg, and white bread crumbs, fry in fat pan and serve on napkin with fried parsley.

## COLD SAUCE ALEXANDER

*(Served at India House with Cold Salmon)*
*For 12 People*

Incorporate into good mayonnaise, chopped chives, parsley, chervil, two tablespoonsful of French mustard and dash of Worcestershire sauce, paprika, pepper and salt; stir well.

# SUPRÊME OF CHICKEN À L'ALEXANDER

Take the breast of a four-pound roasting chicken (stuff very lightly with a filling made of chicken, cream and fresh mushrooms mixed with white of egg) and have it poached in butter and chicken broth. After being done remove the suprême and have the sauce reduced to one-quarter of its volume, then incorporate first one tablespoonful of sweet butter and add six finely chopped French shallots, one-half glass of white wine, two spoonsful of brown sauce (demi-glacé), season well with pepper and salt, let it cook for about three minutes, and strain through fine sieve.

Dish suprême on a fried canape cut to shape and sauce it.

### Garniture

Fried eggplant cut in Julienne shape
Green peppers sauté in butter
Fresh tomatoes sauté

Arrange the vegetables around the suprême on platter by keeping them each separately and serve sauce apart.

## FONDU AU FROMAGE À L'ALEXANDER

Melt two tablespoonsful of butter and work with three spoonsful of flour into light brown color; add one pint of milk, let it boil for five minutes, constantly stirring; incorporate ½ pound of grated Swiss cheese or domestic Roquefort, a little salt and paprika, and bind with six yolks of eggs; let cool down.

This preparation cut and roll into sticks of ¾ inches diameter by 1½ inches long, pass through flour, beaten egg and bread crumbs, and fry crisp in hot fat pan.

Serve in napkin with fried parsley.

## POACHED EGGS EN CROUSTADE À L'ALEXANDER

Work into a dough ½ pound of flour, one tablespoonful of butter, two whole eggs and a little salt; cut this pie-crust dough into tartlette forms, say 3 inches in diameter, place in molds and bake in moderate oven.

Melt two tablespoonsful of fresh butter, add 12 finely chopped shallots, ¼ pound of finely chopped fresh mushrooms, pepper, salt, and let it simmer, by constantly stirring, until it is thoroughly cooked, and finish with chopped parsley; mix well into this two tablespoonsful of demi-glacé. Cover the bottom of tartlettes with a layer of this preparation, place a freshly poached egg on top, cover with thick cream sauce, spray with grated Parmesan cheese, a dash of melted butter, and bake in moderate oven for about five minutes.

Dish up on napkin with crisp fried parsley.

## ROMAINE SALAD À L'ALEXANDER

Decorate half a head of Romaine with sliced grapefruit, sliced orange and white grapes split and seeded, or large black cherries.

Prepare dressing as follows: Incorporate into French dressing finely chopped chives, French mustard and teaspoonful of red currant jelly; mix well and use as dressing for above salad.

## ROGNONS DE VEAU À L'ALEXANDER

Take six fresh veal kidneys, remove skin and fat, and cut to very small cubes, adding ½ pound of very fine chopped fresh mushrooms, and put aside.

Melt two tablespoonsful of butter with twelve finely chopped shallots and brown to a nice golden color. Add the kidneys and mushrooms and let it simmer for about eight minutes, taking good care not to let it cook too much, preventing the kidneys from getting hard; incorporate into this appareil one pint of demi-glacé, one cup of bread crumbs (for thickening) chopped parsley, pepper and salt, and let it cool down.

Cut round canapes of bread 3 inches in diameter, and ½ inch thick, and fry in butter to crusts, and drain; then cover the crusts with this preparation to a half ball shape, pass through beaten egg, spray with a mixture of bread crumbs and grated parmesan cheese and dash of melted butter on top and bake in moderate oven for about ten minutes.

Dish up on napkin with fried parsley, and serve with demi-glacé sauce separate.

# STRAWBERRY TARTLETS ALEXANDER

Work into a dough ½ pound of flour, ¼ pound sugar, 1 tablespoonful of butter, 2 whole eggs, and a little salt.

Cut the dough to oval or round tartlet forms, have them baked in moderate oven, and after they are cooled down fill out the bottom of the tartlets with custard (Crème Patissière). Cover the cream entirely with a layer of selected fresh whole strawberries, and apply, with a decorating brush, lightly diluted red currant jelly; spray the top with finely chopped pistachio nuts.

## BAKED OYSTERS ALEXANDER

Open six large oysters, keep in deep half shell, place in roasting pan and cover with Sauce Alexander as follows:

<blockquote>
two tablespoonsful of Chili sauce<br>
one tablespoonful of horseradish sauce<br>
Mix: one tablespoonful of French mustard<br>
one dash of Worcestershire Sauce<br>
finely chopped chives, salt and pepper
</blockquote>

Take good care the oysters are entirely covered by the sauce, then spray with bread crumbs, and have them baked for about eight minutes.

## ÉMINCE OF CHICKEN À L'ALEXANDER

Select a choice five-pound fowl, have it boiled, cut into flakes and put aside.

Brown in saucepan ¼ pound of butter and two tablespoonsful of flour to a nice yellow color, add to this one quart of chicken broth and let it boil for a few minutes, keeping on stirring it; beat into this sauce six yolks of eggs and the juice of two lemons, working it all the time, but taking good care not to let it boil any more; pass it through a fine sieve and keep it hot in Bain-Marie.

Cut ìnto flakes and sauté in butter ½ pound of fresh mushrooms, then take ¼ pound flaked boiled Virginia ham, one bunch of finely chopped Tarragon and mix this with the chicken flakes in the thoroughly heated sauce; season with salt, pepper and paprika to taste and serve in chafing dish; place on freshly made toast or hot buckwheat cakes.

# XXVI

## Stewart Edward White

## MULLIGAN

This is a camp dish to be cooked over an open fire. I guarantee nothing on a stove. I know nothing of stoves, and have a dark suspicion of them. To make it: Place in a kettle half full of cold water either (a) fish cut in chunks, (b) a couple of dozen clams, or (c) a half dozen chunks of venison about the size of a tennis ball, depending on whether you want a Fish Mulligan, a Clam Mulligan, or a Game Mulligan. Also depending on what you have. Also a half dozen peeled potatoes and three large onions. Salt and pepper, bring slowly to a boil. Add a handful of cubes of salt pork or bacon. Simmer slowly until the potatoes disintegrate. If you have the remains of a can of corn or a little residue of cold rice or anything of like nature, drop them in. Next put in all the stale bread or hard tack the traffic will bear. Dissolve a tablespoonful of flour in a little warm water, and stir that in for thickening. Cook slowly until you can't stand it any longer, and fly to it.

# XXVII

## Oliver Herford

## FRIED ELDERBERRY BLOSSOMS

This sounds like a joke but it is a perfectly serious dish—I made its acquaintance at the table of a little inn in South Baden, on the shores of Lake Constance.

First you must wait until the elderberry bushes are in full bloom. Then you gather a good sized bunch of them—and cut off each blossom just below the point where the little stems join the main stalk.

These you dip into a light egg batter such as is used to make apple fritters (lighter, perhaps), taking care to cover both the flower and as much of the little stalks as possible. They should be served like fritters as soon as made.

# XXVIII

## Reed Smoot

## PEACH COBBLER

One of my favorite dishes is peach cobbler. I am told that it originated in the south, but its fame has spread far beyond the limits of the Mason and Dixon line. It is made in this way:

Line a baking dish or pan, about three and one-half inches deep, with a rich pastry. There must be no break in the pastry. Then fill the dish to the brim with peaches—ripe, luscious ones, that have been pared and broken—not cut—in half. Sugar generously, and leave in about six or eight of the peach pits—they give a certain flavor that only peach pits may impart.

Cover the peaches with an unbroken upper crust of pastry; seal it tightly along the sides, so that none of the juices or aromas may escape. Bake in a slow oven until nearly brown—then sprinkle the top with powdered sugar, that will give a certain professional luster to the dish. After that finish the browning process.

A cobbler containing a quart of peaches should bake for about one hour.

*Editor's Note*:—Senator Smoot is not alone in his partiality toward peach cobbler. Back in the days before Volstead, famous cobblers were produced just as above with the addition of brandy, say a cup to a quart of peaches—but that, of course, was a long time ago.

# XXIX

## Ray Long

### SHAD ROE

Dip the roe well in melted butter or bacon fat, place under hot broiler flame, cooking for five minutes on each side. Then place in a greased baking dish, season with salt, tabasco, Worcestershire sauce and paprika. Dot over with a little more butter, or bacon fat, add a small quantity of hot water, cover closely and bake in an oven until tender—about fifteen minutes. This may be garnished with crisp bacon which should be cooked separately.

### Dessert

Slice fresh pineapple, cover with sugar, and put on ice for several hours. Serve with lemon water ice.

# XXX

## Kenneth C. Beaton

## ("K. C. B.")
## LOBSTER

Get a couple of lobsters.
Split and cleaned.
And put in a pan.
And dot each piece.
With bits of butter.
And put the pan.
In a very hot oven.
And broil ten minutes.
And after that.
Lift meat from shell.
Onto heated plates.
And serve with sauce.
Made in a bowl.
With a bit of mustard.
Stirred in water.
And a pinch of salt.
And of paprika.
Just a dash.
And a scant teaspoon.
Of Walnut catsup.
And a tablespoon.
Of Worcestershire sauce.
And mix them all.
With half a cup.
Of melted butter.
That's just been heated.
And not boiled.
And serve it all.
With a mess of potatoes.
Baked or boiled.
And boy, oh, boy!
There is a dish.
Fit for the gods!
I thank you.

# XXXI

## John Harvey Kellogg, M. D.

### MACARONI WITH CHEESE

1½ cups macaroni
1 cup Cottage Cheese
2 hard boiled eggs
2 tb. butter
2 cups milk or sufficient to cover the macaroni

Boil the macaroni in salt water until tender. Place a layer of macaroni in the bottom of a baking dish, a layer of cheese (½ C.), sliced hard boiled eggs, layer of macaroni and the cheese—bits of butter are placed between the layers and on the top, sprinkle cracker, bread or PEP crumbs over the top, moisten with cream or bits of butter; sufficient milk is poured over to just cover the macaroni and bake in rather a slow oven for about forty-five minutes.

### SAVORY POTATOES

1 pint sliced potatoes
½ small onion
1 tb. butter
1 cup water
1½ teaspoon salt

Place the thin sliced potatoes in the bottom of a baking dish, slice the onion over this and add the remainder of the potatoes; pour hot water over all with butter and salt. Bake in a slow oven two hours.

# XXXII

## Clare Briggs

## WAFFLES

There is a simple but effective recipe for one of the kitchen's most wonderful products.

1¾ cups flour
3 teaspoons baking powder
½ teaspoon salt
1 cup milk
Yolks of 2 eggs
Whites of 2 eggs
1 tablespoon melted butter

Mix and sift dry ingredients; gradually add milk, then yolks of eggs, well beaten. Next the melted butter and last the whites of eggs, beaten stiff. Cook on a very hot and well-greased waffle iron and serve with maple syrup.

Editor's Note:—President Harding favors creamed chipped beef as a dressing for waffles while Mr. Briggs is a staunch supporter of the sweet-tooth school.

For those who like the sweet stuff this variation of plain maple syrup is worth trying:

Put one half pound of strained honey in a double boiler, or a small pan placed in water. Heat very slowly, adding a half pint of pure maple syrup with which has been previously mixed two teaspoons of powdered cinnamon and a dash of caraway. Heat and stir until thoroughly mixed—but do not boil. Serve warm.

# XXXIII

## Edward W. Bok

## ASPARAGUS

The food I like?
The dishes I really crave?
The things off which I would dine every day of my life?
I never see them. I never have them.
Why?
Because Mrs. Bok says there is not a digestible dish amongst them.
But I often think of them,—wistfully, oh, so wistfully!
Here they are:

Soft-shell crabs, done in hot olive oil; or hard-shell crabs; deviled.
Lobster with mayonnaise.
Filet Mignon; panned in brown butter.
Veal loaf.
Roast pork tenderloin.
Fried eels.
Sausages; never had enough; ditto scrapple!
Currants with a hot roll lightly wound through them.
Hot fresh doughnuts.
French pancakes of a thinness like unto gauze.
Strong black coffee.
Chocolate meringue glacé.

But as I never had the good fortune to know the above foods at first hand, I cannot well give you the recipes for them.

Perhaps you might like to know my favorite way of serving asparagus in my home, Dutch fashion, as I remember it in my native land of The Netherlands.

The asparagus bunches are placed in a double boiler upright, the tips being above the water, and thus cooked by steam. Passed at table, with the asparagus, is hard-boiled egg, put through a ricer, a small quantity of finely ground nutmeg and a dish of hot, melted butter. It always has to be explained to guests, but once the introduction is over the convert is made!

39

# XXXIV

## Charles Hanson Towne

## CORN PUDDING

There is no dish I like better than a Corn Pudding made just like this:

2 cups of grated corn
½ cup of milk
½ cup of cream
1 tablespoonful of flour
½ tablespoonful of salt
1 teaspoonful of sugar
1 tablespoonful of butter
A pinch of baking powder

Cook for a half hour and serve immediately. It is brown on the top, and in a deep dish it is the most succulent course a man could wish for. I want others to share it with me. I wish I could give a party every night with this as the pièce-de-résistance!

*Editor's Note:*—In speaking of the origin of this dish Mr. Towne says that it was "first made by my wonderful colored housekeeper, Hattie Jefferson."

# XXXV

## Jerome D. Kern

## TERRAPIN

My favorite dish is Stewed Terrapin and my recipe follows:

Cut the boiled calves' liver into moderate sized pieces and put into stew pan with sufficient fresh butter to stew it well.

In another pan make a sauce of pre-Prohibition Sherry or Madeira, flavored with the beaten yolk of one egg, powdered nutmeg and mace, a pinch of Cayenne pepper, salt to taste, enlivened with large lump of butter.

If pre-Prohibition Sherry is not available, names and addresses of seventy-one bootleggers can be supplied.

Stir sauce well, and just before it comes to a boil, take it off the fire.

Use three or four hard-boiled hens' eggs to pinch hit for turtle's eggs and send to the table piping hot in chafing dish.

*IMPORTANT*: Serve the sauce separately. The terrapin is frequently ignored by those who prefer the flavor of the sherry. I am one of them.

# XXXVI

## Daniel Willard

## COTTAGE PUDDING

One tablespoon butter
One cup sugar
Two eggs
Half cup milk
One large teaspoon baking powder
One and a half cups flour
Bake in a square tin and serve with strawberry sauce.

## STRAWBERRY SAUCE

One large tablespoon of butter beaten to a cream. Add gradually one and a half cups powdered sugar and the beaten white of one egg. Beat till very light and just before serving add one pint of strawberries which have been cut in small pieces.

# XXXVII

## Houdini

## SCALLOPED MUSHROOMS AND DEVILED EGGS

### The Mushroom Dish

Choose for this purpose fine firm ones. Pick, wash, wipe and peel—then lay them in a deep pudding dish well buttered. Season them with pepper and salt, and add a little onion. Sprinkle each layer with rolled bread crumbs, dot with small pieces of butter and proceed in this way until dish is full, having the top layer of bread crumbs. Bake in a moderate oven.

### The Eggs

Boil the eggs hard. Remove shells and cut eggs in half, slicing a bit off the ends to make them stand upright. Extract yolks and rub them to a smooth paste with melted butter, cayenne pepper, a touch of mustard and a dash of vinegar. Fill the hollowed whites with this and send to table upon a bed of chopped lettuce or water cress, seasoned with pepper, salt, vinegar and a little sugar.

# XXXVIII

## Charles P. Steinmetz

## MEAT LOAF

I have been consulted about very many things, but this is the first time I have been consulted on gastronomical matters. But I give herewith, from my camping experience, the following favorite dish of mine:

Beef, veal, and pork (sirloin steak and chops), ½ pound each. Cut off the bones and the fat from the beef and veal, leaving the fat on the pork. Then pass all three through the meat grinder, chopping fairly fine. Add two complete raw eggs and some finely sliced bacon (Beechnut bacon, cut in pieces about 1 inch square) and mix everything together thoroughly, adding the proper amount of salt and pepper and if available some celery salt. Form into the shape of a round loaf.

In a cast iron or cast aluminum frying pan (that is a pan of sufficiently heavy metal to well distribute the heat and guard against local burning) melt some butter, then put the loaf in the melted butter and cover the pan. Heat on a very low fire, turning over after some time, and continue for a long time, until very thoroughly cooked through. Add butter once or twice when absorbed. Then uncover and greatly raise the fire, turning over after a little while so as to brown both sides.

Then take out the loaf and put it on a warm platter or plate. Now pour a cup of cream or rich milk into the pan, stir until the sediment in the pan is dissolved, and heat until you get a good brown gravy. Pour this over the loaf and serve with boiled mealy potatoes. What is left over can be eaten cold, sliced and served on buttered toast.

# XXXIX

## Charlie Chaplin

## STEAK AND KIDNEY PIE

This is how I do it:

Get 2 pounds lean steak
1 beef kidney
1 small onion.

Cut the steak and kidney into two inch pieces. Flour them. Add pepper and salt to taste. Line a deep pie dish with rich pie crust after having buttered dish. Put inverted egg cup in center. Fill with meat and finely chopped onion. Add water almost to top of dish. Roll pastry half inch thick and cover all. Make several small holes in pastry to permit steam to escape. Bake three hours in moderate oven. EAT.

*Editor's Note:*—Steak and kidney pie is a favorite with many beside the great film comedian. Interesting variations of Mr. Chaplin's recipe are:

*Lamb kidney instead of the beef kidney.*
*Top crust only.*
*Fry the meat chunks before putting them into the pie.*

# XL

## Dr. Frank Crane

## ROUND STEAK

Somebody named Johnson, a name with most excellent vibrations, writes me and says that in spite of rumors he has heard, to the effect that I have a hired hand or two to write my stuff, he believes that I honestly wrote all by myself an article which appeared some time ago over my name, in which I stated I could cook round steak so that it would taste as good as fried chicken and be as tender.

"If you are not bluffing," he says, "you could do a world of good to many housekeepers and stag clubs if you would print your recipe. The writer has worn the outer coat of enamel off his teeth in a vain attempt to make himself believe that round steak is as tender as chicken. Give us a hand, pal."

Hence, being called, I lay my cards down, face up, on the table, to wit, namely and as follows:

Have the butcher cut you a round steak thin. A little thicker than a lead pencil. He will insist on cutting it thicker, saying it will be juicier and so on. Draw your revolver and compel him to obey you. Don't have the steak too thick.

After cutting the steak from the piece, have him separate it into portions, each about the size of your hand. Don't try to cook the steak all in one piece. It must be in small sections, just as fried chicken is best when each joint is cooked separately.

Have the butcher then take his sharp knife (which is much better for the purpose than any knife you have at home, because he knows the art of sharpening and you don't), and criss-cross each piece, on both sides, don't forget. So that each piece will be in tatters, almost ready to fall apart.

Put in the frying pan plenty of good sweet lard. Don't use butter. It will burn. Don't fry in deep fat, as with doughnuts, but plenty of fat, as with fried chicken.

Rub each portion of the raw steak in flour. Rub it in good. Drop into the hot skillet. Cover it with lid. Keep covered. This cooks it through and makes it tender.

Fry till a golden brown, turning once in a while. You notice the process is exactly as with fried chicken, Southern style.

After you lift out the meat, put in the flour, let it scorch a bit, then pour water and milk mixed into the hot grease and meat particles left in the skillet. Just how much, you will have to find out by experiment. Let it boil up and boil down, keep stirring, until you have gravy of the right consistency. Flavor according to taste, with salt and pepper, before cooking. If the result is not good it is because you have not followed directions.

Round steak not only is cheap, but it is all good meat, with the minimum of waste, and properly cooked it TASTES better than any part of the beef.

# XLI

## Robert H. Davis

## CREAM SAUCE Á LA WORCESTERSHIRE

This incomparable concoction is to be united in the bonds of holy wedlock with a piece of fried ham, the ceremony to be solemnized on a hot rasher, hooded.

Select a thick slice of mild cured ham, fry it in its own fat in a hot skillet until both sides show a golden brown. Place in a large cooking spoon one spoonful of Worcestershire sauce, and one heaping tablespoon of rich cream. Set the cooking spoon in frying pan beside ham until Worcestershire and cream become warm, adding a few drops of ham fat while the sauce is heating. Complete the perfect union on the rasher by pouring the sauce over the ham.

Put a Mendelssohn Wedding March disc on your phonograph and conclude the honeymoon at the table.

*Editor's Note:*—This sauce was created by Mr. Davis at a breakfast given at the Wyandanch Club, Long Island, by Mr. Charles R. Flint to Admiral Guy Gaunt of the British Navy and Irvin S. Cobb of the United States of America in 1915.

# XLII

## John A. Dix

## FRIED TROUT

For my favorite dish—unhesitatingly—baked beans and pork, country style.

As to my favorite recipe, that requires many condiments, among others a mountain trout stream; the inspiration of the odor of the woods; the vigor of early morning and the pursuit. The requirements, just enough trout plus a few. From the pack basket take a piece of pork or bacon, fry well in a skillet over a carefully laid fire. Prepare the fish and roll well in fine bread crumbs seasoned with salt and pepper. When the fish are done a golden brown remove from the skillet and partake in the aboriginal manner, eating from the fingers. Kings could do no more.

# XLIII

## Guy Bates Post

## LAMB CURRY Á LA "OMAR, THE TENTMAKER"

1 onion (diced)
1 cup of stock
½ cup of rice water
1 cup of potatoes, which have been previously boiled
and diced
2 cups of lamb, cold roast preferred, and cut into the size
of dominoes
2 tablespoons of Curry Powder (Cross and Blackwells, or
other imported—never domestic)
Zest of one lemon
Salt to taste

Give me the above ingredients, and I will make you the meat dish which, above all others, is, to my way of thinking, the most savory and delicious. Eight years ago, when I was first playing "Omar, the Tentmaker," I became acquainted with various members of the Persian Embassy, who were especially interested in the play because of its Persian locale, and it was while dining in the home of one of these gentlemen that I first became initiated to lamb curry—that is, lamb curry as it really should be cooked! Begging the recipe from my host, it has ever since been the favorite pièce-de-résistance in my home.

First of all you brown the onion in olive oil in a deep pan; then add the stock, rice-water, salt and curry powder; the latter having been mixed with a little of the rice-water to insure a smooth sauce. Simmer slowly till the oil and curry float in dark blobs, add the lamb, and continue simmering and stirring until just before serving, when the lemon juice should be dripped in.

Lamb curry should always be served with hot rice, taking on your fork equal portions of both, increasing the amount of rice in case you find the curry too hot. Never drink water with curry, as it intensifies the burning sensation. The amount of curry powder used in the above recipe can be increased or decreased according to the individual taste. Cold cooked shrimps, lobster, veal or chicken may be used in place of lamb; but never beef. Personally I find that lamb produces the finest curry dish.

# XLIV

## Dr. Don Rafael H. Elizalde
## (Minister from Ecuador)

### SANCOCHO

Four pounds of loin beef cut into two-inch squares.
Eight good-sized potatoes.
Five or six ears of green corn, broken in lengths of two inches.
Water sufficient to make the amount of soup required.
Boil until the beef is tender, with the potatoes, then add the corn and cook until done.

*Onions—*

Slice thin three large onions—boil for half an hour, drain and cool. Then pour olive oil over them.

*Banana Paste—*

One quart of milk in a double boiler; add two heaping tablespoonsful of banana flour mixed in a little milk to a smooth paste, and cook from half hour to an hour.

*How to Serve—*

Strain the soup through a colander and serve in a tureen, placing meat, potatoes, corn, onions and banana paste in separate, individual dishes from which each person may help themselves.
(In South America the yucca and plantains are used in this dish.)

### YAPINGACHO

Make potato cakes by the ordinary recipe, but before shaping them place a piece of cream cheese the size of a walnut in the center of each; then fry brown in very little fat.

51

*Sauce—*

One quart of milk and one half pound of peanuts ground fine; boil until thick, seasoning with salt, paprika and butter.

Serve the potato cakes with fried eggs and pour the sauce over both.

# XLV

## Bide Dudley

## TOMATO SOP

Slice firm, ripe tomatoes; roll in flour and fry in equal parts of lard and butter until brown on both sides. Remove several slices to a platter, stir those remaining with flour and small lumps of butter: then thicken with milk and season to taste.

Sop with bread or toast.

*Editor's Note:*—This is good. But in the interest of the culinary art it should be stated that the flour, and not the milk, is the thickening agent.

Try it—you'll thank the author of "tomato sop."

# XLVI

## William Hale Thompson

### (Mayor of Chicago)

### ROAST BEEF

My favorite food is Roast Beef, rare, or a good American sirloin steak, which, I take it, are so simple to prepare that they need no recipe.

### Suggestions:

1. Stand your roast on two or three thin slices of bacon—not too fat.

2. On the top of the roast lay three or four thin slices of lemon—particularly if you like the "outside cut."

3. If your steak looks a bit fresh rub with lemon juice (both sides) and allow to stand several hours before broiling or frying. Don't be frightened if it turns a bit black—be glad.

4. Pan may be rubbed with garlic.

5. Steaks should be thick, particularly if you broil.

# XLVII

## Booth Tarkington

## CORN FLAKES

My favorite dish is corn flakes. They should be placed in a saucer or hollow dish, then lifted in both hands and rolled for a moment, then dropped back into the dish. After that an indefinite quantity of cream should be poured upon them. They should be eaten with a spoon. I don't know how to prepare anything else for the table. I think the best Kennebunkport manner of steaming clams is as follows:

A bushel of clams
4 dozen lobsters
4 dozen ears of sweet corn
4 dozen sweet potatoes
4 dozen eggs

A cartload of seaweed, a bonfire burning for six hours on rocks, then swept away; the lobsters, clams, etc., placed in the seaweed, and the seaweed on the hot rocks and covered with BBB canvas. Allow to steam until screams of distress issue from the seaweed; then be careful what you eat!

# XLVIII

## T. A. Dorgan

## CHILI CON CARNE

*Comes through with a natural*

What is my favorite filler for the feed bag? Well, I'll be on the square with my answer.... It's Chili con Carne.

I might have said Terrapin Maryland, or some other Ritzy dish, but thought I'd better come with a natural.

I'll play Chili con Carne and tamales as they are served in California (where I was born) against any dish I've ever forked over.

### Recipe

Cut, say, two pounds of good beef in small pieces the size of the first finger joint. Add some of the chopped fat, mix and salt.

Put two tablespoonsful of lard in a deep pot and heat. To this add a chopped onion. When the onion is about half cooked add the meat. Stir well until the meat has boiled down in its juice. When it starts to fry add about one and a half pints of hot water, three tablespoonsful of Gebhardt's Eagle Chili Powder and a few buttons of chopped garlic. Simmer and stir well until the meat is tender.

# XLIX

## William De Leftwich Dodge

## RAGOUT DE MOUTON

I think my favorite dish is "Ragout de Mouton," or, I would say, the one I cook the best.

The way it's done is this:

Cut up lamb in small pieces and fry it in a frying pan. Slice three or four carrots and onions and fry them with it. When these are nicely browned, put into a pot, cover with water, and let boil slowly for an hour. Then put in a few potatoes and turnips (cut up in small pieces), and boil until done. Season as you see fit.

# L

## Montague Glass

## BOUILLEBAISSE

Bouillebaisse is my favorite dish. I make it according to the recipe of Valentine Blanc, our cook in Nice, where we lived some years ago. Valentine could neither read nor write, nor could a story tell, but her Bouillebaisse was ever so much better than that they make in Marseilles (and I venture to say in Thackeray's old restaurant either).

Melt about a half pound of butter in a sauce pan. I'm aware that in Marseilles they use oil, but Valentine used butter. Don't let the butter burn. Have ready two large chopped onions—i. e.—onions chopped fine, and two "dents" of garlic also chopped fine.

Cook these in the butter until tender and without burning. Have ready three perch and one haddock. That is to say: cut off the heads and tails. Some people use eels instead of haddock. I detest eels. Cut into a large saucepan the heads and tails of the fish with about a quart of water and let simmer until well cooked, say about half an hour. Strain out the heads and tails and give them to the cat.

Add the cooked onions and garlic,—butter and all—to the strained bouillion from the heads and tails and allow to simmer for half an hour more, after seasoning to taste with salt and white pepper. Add about a gill of dry white wine of any variety,—Chablis, Cotes du Rhone or what not,—the cheaper the wine the better. Now take two smallish lobsters, alive, and if you have the heart, cut them into segments and take off the claws and cut them into segments. Cook the massacred lobster for about a quarter of an hour in the liquid or liquor or bouillon above described and add a saltspoonful of dried Spanish saffron, while the whole is cooking together. If you can get mussels, cook also with the entire mess, a dozen or so,—in their shells if the shells be well scrubbed in advance. Somewhere in this process add about a tablespoonful of chopped parsley. Last of all, add the fish cut into convenient slices rather small, and let cook until done, but not long enough so that the fish becomes disintegrated. Remember there ought to be no violent boiling.

Before serving strain off most of the liquor and serve it first as soup with a slice of toast in the bottom of the plate. If the toast has been fried in advance in good butter, so much the better, but this is

58

not necessary. Then eat all the solid part except the shells and sop up all the remaining gravy with bread, using your fingers to do the job and not a fork. Don't leave a bit of it.

There ought to be enough of this stew for four people, but I can usually manage the whole thing myself with only the slightest assistance from my wife. Wine ought to be drunk with the meal, a good Burgundy Beaune or Chambertin. Later one should eat an artichoke cold vinaigrette, then some fruit and cheese and two small cups of well made black coffee. After this it is necessary to smoke a Corona Corona not too mild, and drink a small glass of Cointreau Sec. The bread ought to be Pain Riche in flutes. The fruit may be fresh apricots, a few green almonds and perhaps some green gages.

The coffee ought to be drunk and the cigar smoked in the garden which must be in the vicinity of Mount Boron on the Grande Corniche or it may be in the Parc Imperial. God ought to be thanked either during or after the meal, and when it becomes a little too cold in the garden a fire should be built in the small living room and one should read Somerville & Ross' Recollections of an Irish R. M., or Neil Lyon's Simple Simon, or Belloc's Path to Rome, or Richard Ford's Gatherings from Spain until bedtime.

Repeat the whole process on the following Friday.

God! How hungry I am.

# LI

## John Philip Sousa

## PELOTAS Á LA PORTUGUESE

*"This serves from six to eight people and is my favorite dish."*

One quart can of tomatoes. Put in kettle on top of stove, simmer or let boil slowly for one and a half hours. Add pepper, salt, two onions cut in fine slices, four allspice and four cloves. The cloves and allspice to be added after it starts to boil. After two and a half hours add:

Two pounds chopped beef; add one onion, chopped fine, two cups bread crumbs, a little parsley, salt and pepper. Make into meat balls about the size of a plum. Put into sauce and boil one and one-half hours slowly. This makes fully three hours' slow boiling for the sauce.

## SPAGHETTI

Use a package or a pound of spaghetti; not macaroni. Have a large pot of boiling water with about one tablespoonful of salt. Slide the spaghetti into the water. Do not break it. Boil exactly twenty minutes. Must be tender, not tough nor doughy.

To sauce, add three bay leaves one hour before taking off the stove.

Serve spaghetti on large platter, pouring tomato sauce over it. Serve pelotas on smaller platter, allowing a small quantity of sauce to remain on them.

Serve grated Parmesan cheese on side. Use a piece of cheese to grate, not bottled cheese.

# LII

## Will Hays

## CHICKEN PILAU

*"Get a fat hen—the fatter the better."*

Because this recipe comes from a Southern cook, there are no accurate measurements.

Sam would always recommend a "fat hen"—"the fatter the better," and "'nough rice and plenty of pepper."

This I know: The chicken is cut up and boiled in the water until tender. Should be cooked in a good sized flat bottom kettle. When the chicken is tender there should be enough of the stock to come up well around it, but not to cover it. Then put in with the chicken about a scant pint of well washed rice. This should be stirred ONCE, Sam says, and allowed to steam slowly an hour. Use plenty of pepper to season and salt to taste. Each grain of rice should be fat and juicy. Successfully made it is delicious.

*Editor's Note:*—The Chicken Pilau recommended by Mr. Hays is delicious. A variation perhaps equally good, may be had by substituting broken spaghetti, or vermicelli for the rice.

# LIII

## Frank Ward O'Malley

## RUM-TUM-TIDDY

*"——has the best Welsh rabbit backed off the stove."*

Take one country home in New Jersey. One dependable apple-jack bootlegger. One cook who threatens to leave unless she can begin her nightly visits to her daughter in the village as early as seven-thirty o'clock.

Take three or four acquaintances who drop in for apple-jack cocktails just as your cook is about to put the steak on to broil. Then have your guests linger near the cocktail shaker until you, your wife and especially your delayed cook are approaching hysteria.

"Why not stay," you now announce to your guests in desperation, "and we'll all make a rum-tum-tiddy?"

You now tell your grateful cook not to bother preparing a meal. You next take one flivver and hurriedly drive her to her daughter's in the village. Then you buy in the village one and one-half pounds of American cheese, one can of Campbell's Tomato Soup and a dozen bottles of beer—real beer, if you can get it, Volstead beer if you can't.

*NOW:—*

Pry your guests away from the cocktail shaker and shoo them into the kitchen. Everybody from this on who is not occupied in mincing the green pepper in a chopping bowl is busy cutting the American cheese into cubes about an inch square. Everybody else beats two fresh eggs—whites and yolks together.

Drop a lump of butter into a saucepan to prevent "sticking." Begin to melt the pound and one half of diced cheese in the saucepan, stirring the lumps to prevent burning. When the cheese is fairly well melted, pour into it the can of tomato soup and the two beaten eggs. Stir into the mixture about one-third of a bottle of beer. Pour in also the finely chopped green pepper and continue stirring until smooth.

Have hot dinner plates ready, each plate containing a large

62

slice of hot, unbuttered toast. Place at least one bottle of beer—two if it's real—beside each plate.

Holler "Ready, people!" and pour on each piece of toast enough of the contents of the saucepan to form a pinkish overflow of rum-tum-tiddy on the plate.

That's all—except to shake 'em up a semi-final cocktail and then start right back to the village in the flivver for another pound and one half of cheese, another pepper and more beer to make another immediately when the first rum-tum-tiddy is gone. One calls for two, often three.

Serve preferably in the kitchen. Serve in any room far from the kitchen if you want leg work exercise. Eat until gorged.

# LIV

## Charles Evans Hughes

## CORN BREAD

*"My favorite dish is corn bread and honey."*

And here is a recipe for corn bread:

2 cups of flour
3 cups of cornmeal
4 heaping teaspoonsful of baking powder
2 eggs well beaten
1 teaspoonful salt
1 tablespoonful sugar
1 pint of milk
2 tablespoonsful of melted butter

Mix the meal and flour, baking powder, salt and sugar. Beat the eggs until they are light, then add the eggs and milk to the meal. Beat to a light smooth consistency and add the melted butter. Bake in a shallow pan (greased) for about twenty-five minutes.
Eat while hot and use plenty of fresh butter and honey.

*Editor's Note:*—There is a white meal and a yellow. Expert appraisers of corn bread have said that the white meal is preferable. Still the golden hue of a pan of hot corn bread is not to be passed up lightly.

# LV

## Walter Prichard Eaton

## MINCE-PIE

"Made any other way it's not mince-pie."

My favorite dish, and the best food in the world, is King Canute Pudding, but I shall not tell anybody how to make it, because that is a family secret. I am descended from Canute, and this was the pudding he ate and which made him feel so good that he went out and bade the tide to cease rising. The recipe is handed down in each generation of my tribe. It was my paternal grandmother who had it to pass on. She lived to be ninety-nine, thanks to her own wonderful cooking and a cantankerous disposition. Her mince-pie was a thing to write sonnets about. It was the second best food in the world. For ten years after I went to New York I lived on the memory of that pie and shuddered at the horrendous messes masquerading under the same name which were offered to me.

Then I moved back to New England and achieved a cook who, by the grace of God and the right bringing up could make a pie like it. For six years I knew happiness again. Then we lost Kate, the incomparable. My only hope was my wife and that was a feeble hope, indeed. She was born not in the pie belt, but in New York. She had never cooked. She was an Episcopalian. I approached the next Thanksgiving breakfast with gloomy forebodings.

But lo, a miracle. It was an orthodox mince-pie. It was Katie's mince-pie. It was grandmother's mince-pie—in short, it was mince-pie. Here is the way to make it. Made any other way it's not mince-pie.

### The Filling

Affix the grinder firmly to the edge of the table. What the palette is to the artist so is the grinder to the creator of mince meat. Then pass the following ingredients through the grinder, and from thence into a large kettle and let the latter and its glorious contents simmer on the stove for the best part of a morning, stirring them frequently so that no portion shall be neglected and fail to come into close union with the soothing heat that mellows all into one fragrant

65

whole. Take from the stove and store in stone crocks or glass jars in the dark, and keep tightly covered. When about to fashion a pie take out as much of the meat as you desire, wet it with boiled cider and with fresh cider, too, if possible, so that it is not stiff, and bake between the crusts whose ingredients are given below. Eat hot with soft dairy cheese and coffee.

The meat should be thoroughly boiled the day before the mince meat is made, and the cider should be boiled down at home—not bought—until it is the consistency of molasses. Boil enough to last all winter and put in glass jars. Now, alas, that no liquors may be had, it is well to bottle fresh cider and put it away where it is cool, so that with luck it may still be fresh when in March you scrape the last jar for the last pie. Only use care when it is opened, or perchance it will be the ceiling rather than the pie which will be wet down.

5 cups cooked beef; after grinding
2½ cups suet
7½ cups apples
3 cups cider
½ cup vinegar
1 cup molasses
5 cups sugar
¾ pound citron
2½ pounds raisins
1½ pounds small raisins (not to be put through grinder)
salt to taste
juice and rind of 2 lemons
juice and rind of 2 oranges
1 tablespoon mace and nutmeg (or 2 nutmegs grated)
2 tablespoons each of cinnamon, cloves and allspice
2 tablespoons lemon extract
1 teaspoon almond extract
3 cups liquor in which beef was cooked

If you have wine or brandy put in a cupful after taking from the fire.

### The Crust

2 cups pastry flour sifted with teaspoon salt.
½ cup (generous) of lard mixed in with fingertips till the combination is fine and powdery.
Wet with cold water, mixing with knife, and cutting, till you

can take the dough from the bowl without sticking to it. Divide in half, pat gently on floured marble slab, and roll out thin. Lift lower crust carefully, place in tin and trim off edges. Roll out from trimmings a strip half an inch wide and place on top of lower crust, around edge, first wetting edge slightly with cold water. Put in filling, place upper crust on top, first wetting edge of rim slightly with cold water, press together with tines of fork and trim off overhanging of upper crust. Prick a large T. M. on the top crust and bake in hot oven till brown.

(The T. M. stands for "'Tis Mince" to distinguish it from the pies labeled T. M. for "'Tain't Mince.")

# LVI

## W. T. Benda

## POLISH SPECIALTIES

In following my Polish recipes you will find a practical use for the geometry of your school days. If you have forgotten the axioms of Euclid, take a correspondence course before attempting "Ushka."

It is simple when you finally master it—and marvelously good. Don't forget the line B D. Everything hinges on that.

## BARSHCK WITH USHKA

### Barshck. (Or Polish Beet Soup)

If you are brave, put three large beets, peeled and quartered into a glass jar and pour on them a quart of water, add a teaspoonful of salt and a slice of rye bread. Keep this in a warm place for about five days. There will form a sour red-wine-like juice with a whitish mold skin on the top. Don't lose your courage, take this skin off and pour off the juice.

Then prepare a quart of beef, pork and vegetable stock and while it is hot add to it all your beet juice and a bottle of cream which you previously have beaten with a teaspoonful of flour. Heat and stir it all just to boiling point, but do not let it boil, and serve with or without "Ushka" which are fully described in the next paragraph.

### Ushka

Barshck is really not complete without "Ushka," and as they are a very simple dish to prepare you should never omit them.

To make "Ushka" prepare first a fine hash of half a pound of boiled pork and beef with one small onion, a tablespoonful of flour, salt and pepper.

68

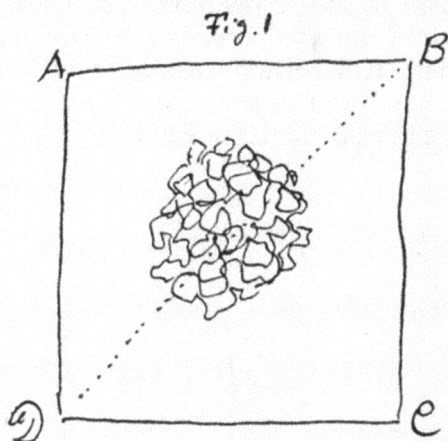

Fig. 1

Make white sauce of butter and flour and a little water, mix this with your hash, let it stew for a while, then add one raw egg and stir it madly.

Now mix a dough, using half a quart of flour, one egg, two tablespoonfuls of water, half a teaspoonful of salt, and butter of the size of a walnut. Knead this vigorously for half an hour, or until it is quite smooth.

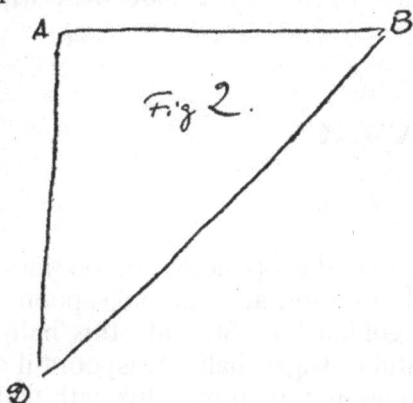

Fig. 2

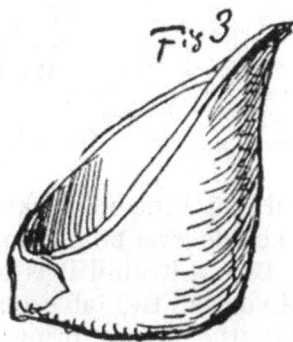

Fig. 3

Roll the dough out into a sheet 1/8 of an inch thick and cut it into 2½ inch squares. Put on each dough square a teaspoonful of your hash; fold them diagonally along the line BD (Fig. 1) and press the edges together, thus joining the edge AB unto the edge CB and AD unto CD. You will thus obtain the right angle triangle ABD (Fig.

69

2) with the hash inside. Now curve this triangle along the hypotenuse BD until the 45 degree corner D meets the 45 degree corner B. Let these two corners overlap a little and press them together until they stick. The shape resulting from this operation resembles a pig's ear, as depicted in Figure 3.

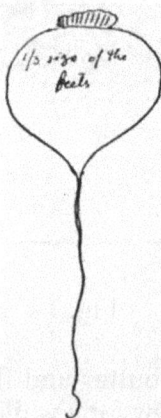

1/2 size of the feels

Now put these pig's ears or Ushka into boiling water; they will sink, but that should not distress you. Leave them there until they come to the surface. Put the Ushka on a platter and pour on them brown butter with crumbs and serve them as a side dish with barshck.

## BURACHKI

### (Beets à la Polonaise)

Boil eight little beets, skin them and chop them (not too fine).
Take one level tablespoonful of butter, and one tablespoonful of flour. Brown it until it is of a golden hue. Stir into this half a cupful of vinegar, two tablespoonsful of sugar, half a teaspoonful of salt and a little pepper. Bring it to boiling, then mix this with your beets.

70

# LVII

## Captain Edward A. Salisbury

### SAUCE FOR SPAGHETTI

This sauce for spaghetti is a real Italian mixture—and wonderful. This is how I learned to make it in Italy:

Place in a cup or bowl a half teacup full of dried mushrooms. Pour boiling water over them and just let them stand until thoroughly softened, say—about a half hour.

In the meantime cover the bottom of your frying pan or skillet with butter or olive oil (I prefer the butter). Chop one big onion and cook slowly, stirring frequently. In another pan or kettle place two cans of tomatoes. Stew them for half an hour. Then make three small cakes of Hamburg steak or chopped beef and put them in to cook, with the onions. Cook thoroughly. Add at the same time the mushrooms which have been softened and chopped into fine particles.

When the meat is cooked through mash the cakes up with a fork—mixing well with onions and mushrooms.

Now add the stewed tomatoes and, in doing this, press them through a sieve or colander. Stir well.

Place on back of stove and let steep for one hour after adding two teaspoons of Eagle Chili Powder (if available) or two teaspoons of Lea & Perrins sauce with five dissolved cubes of beef or chicken bouillon.

To cook the spaghetti, place it, unbroken, in well salted boiling water. Put it in end first. Boil exactly twenty-three minutes. Drain. Hold under cold water tap for a second or two and drain again. Keep warm on stove until served. This cold water treatment is important. It removes all gumminess and leaves the spaghetti in perfect condition. Use the imported spaghetti if available.

### EGGS À LA SALISBURY

Here is a dish that is easy to make and delicious.

I poach the desired number of eggs until they are just solid.

71

Then I place them on hot, crisp toast, covering the eggs with beautifully done bacon.

Over the lot, I pour hot cream until the eggs are floating.

Salt, pepper and paprika to taste.

Try this for breakfast.

## FISH À LA COMMODORE

Say you are cooking a six pound bass or some similar fish—do it this way for a change:

Rub the fish well with salt and pepper. Don't be afraid to rub. Then open the flesh in three places and insert in each opening a clove of garlic.

Next slice six large onions—six small green peppers—and six large tomatoes. Now take your Dutch oven or baking pan and cover the bottom with Mazola oil or olive oil—add a tablespoon of butter.

When this is hot put in your fish and cover the fish with the sliced vegetables. Salt and pepper the vegetables.

Cook until the vegetables are done or about one hour. Baste frequently to avoid scorching the vegetables. To the basting add two teaspoons of Lea & Perrins sauce and one-half wine glass of cooking Sherry when half done.

When serving put plenty of juice and sauce on each portion and make them come back for more. This recipe can be used for many kinds of large fish.

## TO COOK TROUT

Dip trout in beaten egg, salt and pepper. Roll in flour and drop into very hot and very deep Mazola oil. Remove when golden brown. The trout will be perfectly free from oil and every bit of the delicate trout flavor will be sealed up inside. Try it!

## VENISON STEAK

Venison steak is fairly poor steak at best. But there is one way to cook it that makes you forget all past experiences with venison.

And remember this is really the only way to cook it that's worth a damn.

Take the venison and strip out all of the white sinews that lay between the muscles or lean parts. Strip and cut this white part all away. Then cut your venison into small strips about the thickness of a finger. Now you are on your way. Beat up an egg or two and beat in a bit of salt and pepper. Dip your strips of venison in the egg, then roll them in flour. Fry in butter and serve immediately.

Every hunter or guide who has tried this sticks to it. It's the one way to cook venison.

## GOOSE

There is only one way for a man, or any one else, to cook a goose. Listen: Never pick a goose! Just pull the skin right off—every inch of it.

Then take a sharp knife and follow down the breast bone on both sides. Strip the breast meat clear away from both sides. Split each side of breast into two thin steaks (if large goose).

Dip these steaks in beaten egg, salt and pepper. Roll in flour and fry over a medium fire. That's new to most folks for goose and it's going to give you a new idea about geese when you try it.

## A MAYONNAISE AND A SALAD DRESSING

Take yolks of two eggs, beat well and add slowly (drop at a time) olive oil. If your mixture is too thick lighten with dash of lemon or vinegar.

Now into a half pint of this mayonnaise put three tablespoons of Chili sauce; three tablespoons of Blue Label Ketchup; one tablespoon of finely chopped pimento; one tablespoon of finely chopped blanched sweet peppers.

To this add one-half teaspoon of salt—pepper and Hungarian paprika to taste.

Then add, slowly, Tarragon vinegar to taste—say about one and one-half tablespoons.

Serve this on shrimps, lobster, lettuce or tomato salad.

# DUCKS AND LARGE FOWL

Ducks, such as Mallard, Canvasback and Redhead, should be baked. If you once learn how to bake in a Dutch Oven you have found the secret of successful camp cookery.

Take a Mallard, for instance. Rub it with salt and pepper (I might add here: pick 'em dry and keep 'em dry—no water near a duck!), then put an onion well up in the body cavity. Fill the remaining space with celery, wild or domestic.

Get your oven, or Dutch oven, very hot before the duck goes in. Use no grease and no water—just your dry pan or oven. A big Mallard will cook perfectly in twenty minutes. Do not open oven or take lid from Dutch oven after starting to cook. Serve with currant jelly.

## TEAL, PARTRIDGE AND SMALL FOWL

Pick, without breaking the skin. Cut open the back and break out flat for grilling or broiling. Broil bone side to the fire for eight minutes. Souse frequently with melted butter.

Turn and broil, flesh side to the fire, for four minutes, using more butter. Salt and pepper thoroughly at time of turning.

Serve with currant jelly.

## BEANS

Get a deep pot for beans. A heavy iron one is mighty good.

Take a half pound of salt pork and cut it into very small pieces. Fry them until brown.

Clean your beans and soak them for at least two hours—or more. Then boil the beans for two hours, after which add the pork and one can of Mexican Chili Sauce. If this is not available, make your own by frying with the salt pork: four tomatoes, three onions, two bell peppers and one red pepper, all chopped.

Now you've got your mixture and after it's all together put in six beef bouillon cubes; salt and pepper to taste.

It's a good idea to have enough water in the pot so that when the beans are done a fine soup may be enjoyed before the beans are eaten. Altogether three to four hours of cooking is necessary for the best results with beans.

## ITALIAN RICE

First, a word about cooking rice. Buy the best head rice. Wash it thoroughly,—six waters. Drop rice slowly into well salted, boiling water, and boil for twenty-three minutes. Drain off three-quarters of water and hold rice under cold water faucet for a moment; this will leave each grain firm and perfect. Drain thoroughly.

Now the sauce. Place in your skillet olive oil to cover the bottom; also tablespoon of butter. Chop one large Spanish onion. Place it in the skillet and cook slowly. Stir often.

After ten or fifteen minutes, a piece of white fish (sole preferred) about the size of your four fingers, from the palm down— see? When the onions are a golden color add one finely chopped clove of garlic. When fish is thoroughly cooked, mash it up with a fork and stir well. Now add one or two cans of tomatoes which have been stewing slowly for half an hour or more. Add them through a sieve and push with a spoon so as to get the thick part through. Mix well.

Place this on the back of the stove where it will simmer for one hour. Add a pinch of saffron or thyme—salt and pepper to taste.

This sauce can be used for only one meal, as it sours after a few hours. Sauce should be applied by each person as desired until it's all gone.

## STEAK SAUCE

Have a large platter very, very hot—really hot!

Then the minute the steak is done, put it on the platter and work fast. Over the steak sprinkle a very little bit of dry English mustard. Then a squeeze or two of lemon. Now several thin slices of butter, a little Worcestershire sauce, salt, pepper and paprika. Rub all this in with a broad knife. Turn steak and repeat the operation. Now tip platter on edge and quickly whip the sauce into a froth, using a fork. Serve two or three tablespoons of sauce with each piece of steak.

# LVIII

## Thomas H. Ince

## CHICKEN HALIBUT

### *(Baked and with Parmesan)*

Boil some slices of halibut in court bouillon, lay in baking dish a border of potato croquette—either hard or shaped with hand. Have layer of bechamel on bottom of dish—then one of shredded fish, another layer of bechamel and one more of fish, finishing with the bechamel; sprinkle with bread crumbs and grated Parmesan. Pour over a little butter and brown in the oven.

With Parmesan. Prepare same and make solid paste by mixing together butter and Parmesan cheese with pinch paprika. Work well and roll out one-eighth inch thick. Cover last layer bechamel with this and brown in hot oven.

Bechamel Sauce. Prepare roux of butter and flour, let cook few minutes while stirring—not allow to color—remove to slower fire and leave it to cook 15 minutes. Then dilute gradually with half boiled milk.

## ONION SOUP AU GRATIN

Cut into small 1/8 inch squares two medium onions, fry them in butter and add two dessert spoons flour and moisten with two quarts of broth, adding bunch of parsley garnished with chervil, bay leaf and clove and garlic. Season with a little salt, pepper and some meat extract, boil for 20 minutes—then remove the bouquet—pour the soup over very thin slices of bread placed in a metal soup tureen in intervening layers of bread and cheese—Parmesan—finishing with the Parmesan and sprinkle a little over the top of the soup. Bake in hot oven or boil ten minutes and thicken with raw yolks of two eggs diluted in cream.

# RICE Á LA MANHATTAN

Chop two onions—fry in butter, add a pound of rice and beat together. When very hot, add enough broth to triple quantity—let boil and cook in slack oven for 20 minutes. Add when done, six ounces grated Parmesan. Pour ⅔ of this into casserole, make hole in center and fill with shrimps and minced mushrooms; around sides lay fillet of sole, pour over lean Spanish sauce—reduced with essence of mushrooms—mix well and cover whole with remainder of rice—put in hot oven for fifteen minutes and serve.

Sauce:—1 quart of stock—melt ¼ pound of butter—stir in same amount of flour—making clear paste—add stock—brown slowly.

# LIX

## George Ade

## "SCOLLOPED" OYSTERS

If I must make a decision, I think I shall have to vote in favor of escalloped oysters. Back home we call them "scolloped." The restaurant and hotel article is not the real thing. The portions are stingy and the oysters are heated just enough to render them helpless and they lie embedded in some dry packing, evidently meant to be an article of food. Escalloped oysters, as prepared at home, came in a deep pan which had been subjected to great heat. The oysters were used with the greatest prodigality. They were cooked in cracker crumbs or corn meal and they were cooked until the delicious flavor of the bivalve had permeated all parts of the dish. Milk or cream and real country butter had been used unsparingly, so that the whole compound was moist and the seasoning had been well distributed, and the whole result was, in my opinion, a triumph. For some reason, the real "scolloped" oysters attain their perfection only when prepared by women past thirty years of age.

I am not undertaking to give the recipe. Probably it is something secret—beyond the reach or comprehension of any man, but the dish itself is worthy of all the complimentary adjectives.

*Editor's Note:*—Here is the way to do it—first butter the bottom and sides of a pan (deep) or baking dish, then cover the bottom with those little, round, old-fashioned oyster crackers, all crisp and salty. Next place a layer of oysters, fresh or cove. If you don't know what cove oysters are ask some one who was raised in the Middle West. Now a layer of crackers crushed; then more oysters and so on until the pan is full. Season each layer of oysters with salt and pepper. Put little bits of butter all over the cracker layers. Now fill the pan with milk and cream to which has been added a bit of the oyster liquor. Cover the top well with crushed crackers. Put a cover on the dish or pan and slip it into the oven. Some folks add a teaspoonful of Worcestershire sauce to the milk and cream. Bake until the juices bubble up. Don't let too much of the moisture bake away. At the last minute take the cover off the dish and brown the top.

The richer the cream and butter the better the result.

The dish is even better than Mr. Ade would lead you to believe, and it can be made by an amateur male cook—that's why Mr. Ade's contribution is printed in spite of the rank heresy to which he professes.

# LX

## Lyman Abbott

## DEEP APPLE PIE

Dr. Lyman Abbott's favorite dish is a Deep Apple Pie, which is made like the deep fruit tarts so plentiful in England.

Here is a thoroughly satisfactory way to make Dr. Abbott's specialty: Line a deep pie tin with a rich crust, fill with tart, juicy apples sliced very thin. Sprinkle sugar and a little cinnamon over them. Scatter bits of butter over the apples, about a tablespoonful in all. Also sprinkle with a tablespoonful of water. Use four or five tablespoonsful of sugar. Cover with top crust and bake slowly for a half, or perhaps three-quarters of an hour.

For the real deep dish pie put the apples, sugar and butter (above proportions) in the individual deep dish and cover with top crust. Bake the same. The spices may be varied to taste.

# LXI

## Terry Ramsaye

## LETTUCE (à la Red Creek)

In behalf of my favorite fodder, the tender leafling lettuce that's newly sprung in June, I am pleased to present a method of introducing it to the human system with a maximum effectiveness.

Wilted Lettuce:—It is said that this dish comes to us from the Hessians. If this be treason let us make the most of it.

Having obtained the lettuce, young and tender and fresh from the patch, plucked before it is yet headstrong, toss it into a bucket of cold water to crisp it.

Repairing to the kitchen, place on the hot stove a skillet and heave into it a good sized cupful of chopped bacon. Let it fry thoroughly. Add a dessert spoonful of salt, a pinch of mustard, a couple of tablespoonsful of granulated sugar and good cider vinegar in quantity slightly in excess of the bacon fat. Let it simmer smartly until well blended. Meanwhile lay out the lettuce in noble heaps on the plates on which it is to be served. Chop up a handful of green onions, a bit of the tops will do no harm, and at the last moment stir them into the concoction in the skillet.

While the whole is sizzling and boiling vigorously, pour the mixture over the lettuce, using a spoon to apportion the nifty bits of bacon about, and serve forthwith.

By this method one can take aboard amazing quantities of lettuce, which is most desirable in view of the fact that this gentle herb contributes strongly to the summer languor when taken in adequate quantities.

# LXII

## R. L. (Rube) Goldberg

## HASH

All joking aside, my favorite dish is hash.

I have never actually been in the kitchen to see hash pass through the various stages of its epicurean development, but I imagine hash is manufactured something like this:

First the father must eat a big lunch, the mother must fill herself up on cake in the afternoon and the children must have spoiled stomachs. This condition of affairs ruins the evening meal completely and there is plenty of meat left over for hash the next day.

The cook takes the beef or veal or whatever it is and throws it into the electric fan. The flying bits of meat are caught on ping pong rackets by experts and knocked back into a pot that contains a large quantity of mashed potatoes. Then the fire is lighted and the cook can go out to an afternoon movie.

The beauty of hash is that, no matter how it tastes, you think it is all right. There is no standard flavor for hash. Hash is fundamentally accidental, so it has no traditions to live up to.

# LXIII

## Channing Pollock

## CORN BREAD

When I was young and sometimes went camping my favorite dish was corn bread. In those days, we always began proceedings by building a mud oven. Now I believe portable ovens are convenient and cheap. In any event, following is my recipe:

> 2 cups of flour
> 3 cups of cornmeal
> 4 heaping teaspoonsful of baking powder
> 2 eggs well beaten
> 1 teaspoonful of salt
> 1 tablespoonful of granulated sugar
> 1 generous pint of milk
> 2 tablespoonsful of melted crisco or lard
> Do not scald the cornmeal.

Mix the meal with flour, baking powder, salt and sugar, beat the eggs until they are light, add the milk and eggs to the other ingredients. Beat the whole until it is smooth and light—about one minute. Finally adding the melted crisco or lard; pack into shallow, greased pan and bake in a hot oven for twenty-five minutes.

# LXIV

## Hussein Kahn Alai

### (Minister to the United States from Persia)

## CHIRIN POLOW

Necessary materials: One pound of rice (Carolina rice is most suitable); one spring chicken; the peel of four oranges; four ounces of sugar; half a pound of salt; two grams of Spanish saffron; two ounces of almonds; half a pound of butter.

Method of cooking the rice: If the dish is required for a luncheon at one o'clock, it will be necessary, the night before, to rinse the rice three times in water, rubbing it each time with the palms of the hands. Change the water each time.

Next soak the rice in tepid water, letting the water stand three inches over the rice. Pour the half pound of salt on the rice and let it stand until 11 a. m. of the next day.

Into a two gallon caldron pour six quarts of water and let it boil. As soon as it boils pour out slowly and with care the water in which the rice has been soaking since the night before. Empty the rice into the boiling water. Cover the caldron and increase the heat. As soon as the caldron containing the rice begins to boil remove the cover and stir the rice gently with a flat spoon. Then replace the lid and let the contents of the caldron boil again. Repeat the stirring process three times. Next drain the rice in a sieve, shaking it to remove all adherents of salt and starch. Now melt a quarter of a pound of butter in a large cup of water. Pour half of the melted butter into a one-gallon caldron and gently empty the rice into the caldron in such a way that it will spread uniformly without sticking together in rice balls. Place the caldron in a hot oven. Close the oven and after five or six minutes see if the caldron is hot; if it is, bring it out gently and pour the remainder of the melted butter over the rice and replace in the oven. Now reduce the heat until the caldron gives a hollow sound when rapped with the fingers; this will indicate that the rice is sufficiently cooked.

Preparation of the almonds: Boil the almonds for a few minutes until the skins fall off and the almonds become white. Cut the almonds into four quarters perpendicularly.

84

Preparation of the orange peel: Remove the white part of the peel to such an extent that both sides of the peel are of the same color. When this has been done cut the peel into long thin strings. These should be boiled in two waters so as to remove all bitterness. Then strain.

Combining the almonds and the orange peel: Mix the almonds and the orange peel and boil them in a syrup of sugar for ten minutes. Strain and keep in a warm place until needed.

Cooking the chicken: Begin boiling the chicken very slowly at eight o'clock in the morning. Boil to such a point that the skin and bones detach themselves from the flesh.

Preparation of the saffron: Warm the saffron to remove all dampness and pound it to a powder in a mortar; after which dissolve it in three tablespoonsful of cold water.

Dishing the Polow: One half of the rice should be taken from the caldron and mixed in a bowl with the orange peel and almonds. Over this sprinkle three tablespoonsful of saffron water to color well. Now pour over it about two tablespoonsful of melted butter.

Next remove the remainder of the rice from the caldron and dish it up ready for the table. Place the chicken from which the skin and bones have been removed on top of the rice. Crown the whole with the rice, which has already been mixed with the almonds and orange peel and colored with the saffron.

This will make a delightful and pleasantly flavored dish— Chirin Polow, which means "sweet Polow."

# LXV

## William J. Bryan

## FRENCH-FRIED ONIONS

Onions are on my permitted list of foods and they are prepared for the table in many ways. The best way that I know of has been given the name of French-fried onions. I first ate onions in this form at the famous Grove Park Inn, Asheville, North Carolina, and have since introduced the dish on dining cars and into many private homes.

Take a Bermuda onion—any other large onion would do—cut it into slices through the rings so that each slice will be made up of a large number of whole rings. Then break the slices up into separate rings, drop these into a thin batter and fry them as you fry French-fried potatoes. Each ring looks like a little doughnut. I find that the dish is universally praised.

May I add a word in regard to radishes, of which I am very fond. The long White Icicle radish is, in my judgment, the best variety and I have found that butter added to the salt makes the radish a little more palatable.

# LXVI

## Will Irwin

## HAM AND EGGS

Take a frying pan and some ham. Cook the ham in its own fat in the frying pan—cook until the ham is well dappled with golden brown, or until it is cooked enough. Then break some eggs. Take out the ham and put it on a hot platter, then put in the eggs. Baste them a bit with the hot ham fat. Put a cover on the pan and let the eggs cook in the hot pan with no fire. A minute or two will do—then serve the eggs with the ham and—oh, boy!

For the very best results use the best ham you can get and plenty of day old eggs.

# LXVII

## Douglas Fairbanks

## BREAD TART

1 cup fresh bread crumbs
1 cup sugar
1 cup chopped nut meats
1½ teaspoons baking powder
5 eggs
2 tablespoons grape juice
1 lemon

### Filling

1 egg
½ cup chopped walnut meats
½ cup sugar
½ cup lemon

Soak bread crumbs with grape juice and the strained lemon juice. Beat egg yolks and sugar together until light; then add nut meats, baking powder, bread crumbs and the beaten whites of the eggs. Divide into buttered and floured layer tins and bake in a moderate oven for twenty minutes. Put together with filling. Beat up egg, add sugar, lemon juice and walnuts. This tart may be covered with frosting if liked.

# LXVIII

## Julian Street

## SOLE Á LA MARGUERY AND DUCK WITH ORANGES

I have two favorite dishes: both being examples of the French cuisine at its highest.

One is "Sole à la Marguery" (which can be made with flounder, also) and was originated by old Monsieur Marguery at his famous restaurant in Paris. It has a sauce which has a wine base and which contains shrimps and small oysters.

### Sole à la Marguery

Lay your sole in a buttered platter, add about a glassful of white wine, season and poach:

I. E. Let boil for about fifteen minutes and then take the juice out, mix with it a yolk of a raw egg, about two ounces of sweet butter. Beat slowly so as to get it thick, something like a hollandaise; add a few shrimps, oysters, mussels, and a few heads of mushrooms, cook the sole with it, glaze in a salamande two or three minutes and serve.

Another is duck cooked with oranges. I know how to ask for it at the St. Regis and the Brevoort, but am not sure of the spelling. It sounds like Duck "Bigarade." They do it well at the Brevoort. If potatoes are served with either of these dishes they should be potatoes gaufrettes—on a separate plate.

### Duck Bigarade

To Roast: Select a young and very tender duck, prepare and truss it for roasting. It should be roasted on the spit or in the oven for fifteen to twenty-five minutes, according to its size and the heat of the fire.

A domestic duck ought to be served quite rare, and should be killed without bleeding. Dish it after untrussing and pour over it a little of its gravy.

Sauce Bigarade: Peel an orange without touching the

89

white parts, cut the peel up into small, fine julienne. Plunge it into boiling water, and cook until it is tender. Drain and enclose it in a covered saucepan with four gills of espagnole or brown sauce. Just when ready to serve finish the sauce with a dash of cayenne pepper, meat glaze, the orange juice and the juice of a lemon, strain through a tamis, adding two ounces of fine butter.

# LXIX

## S. S. McClure

## OMELETTE—AND PIE

I can give you a tip on how to prepare, in the very best fashion, two articles of food.

The first is omelette: The frying pan should be held at a slant, with the lower part immediately over a moderate heat, and continually the volume of eggs that becomes cooked should be scraped back and the liquid part allowed to flow over the pan thus emptied, and then when the omelette is, I should say, about two-thirds cooked, it should be removed from the fire and dished.

It is impossible to make an omelette of the utmost symmetry and firmness and have it good at the same time. If it is stiff enough to maintain a certain symmetry, then it is too stiff to be good. I have made an omelette in this fashion containing as many as eighteen eggs. I learned how to make omelette from Madame Poulard of Mont St. Michel in Normandy, one of the most famous omelette makers in Europe.

I am also particularly successful in making pies. On one occasion I made pies for one hundred and eighty-five officers on the troop-ship Leviathan. To make pies, one must have the best quality of butter and the best quality of flour. Use a pound of butter to every two pounds of flour. The butter must be rather firm and must be mixed with the flour with your hands. Then when you have a sort of a mass of dough on the table, make a little hollow in the middle, pour in a little cold water, mix it to such a consistency that it can be made into a roll perhaps as thick as your wrist. It will require about two inches to be rolled out thin for the crusts. Dust a little flour in the dish that it is to be baked in and put into the oven at such a temperature as would require one half an hour to bake. There's a considerable secret in the choice of fruits. The top crust should have little apertures in it so as to permit the steam to escape. It is easier to make perfect pies than any other dish.

# LXX

## Basil King

## LOBSTER Á LA KING

Boil medium sized lobsters. Let grow cold and remove meat. Put large piece of butter and one and one-half tablespoons of flour into double boiler. Stir until creamy. Add one pint of milk and cook about five minutes. Add lobster cut in small pieces and cook about fifteen minutes. Just before serving; add three tablespoons cream and one-half tumbler sherry or brandy.

*Note:* Unless brandy or sherry can be added it is useless to attempt this dish.

# LXXI

## John A. Moroso

## SPAGHETTI-FOR-THE-GANG

Many a time as a very small boy I watched my distinguished Piedmontese grandfather grandly direct the cook. This is the way our spaghetti sauce was prepared. Buy about three or four pounds of solid meat from the round, cut thick. Ask for the "eye of the beef." It is inexpensive. Cut little pockets in it and insert bits of fat bacon in some. In others stuff sage, thyme, parsley and bay leaf with salt and pepper to taste. Sometimes I spread thinly with mustard, the prepared sort; covering the top. A clove of garlic tucked in with the seasoning goes well, if you have Wop ancestry. Pale people use onions. But surely one or the other.

Grease well a deep iron skillet with iron top, the pot-roast utensil. When the gravy begins to drip add a little water, but not much. The steam makes the meat tender and brings out all the flavors in the little pockets. Baste from time to time just to get the aroma of the simmering mess and sharpen your appetite. Take a little wire and jab it in the roast after about an hour and twenty minutes and you'll find out whether it is tender and juicy enough.

Put the big pot on and get your water boiling fast. Add a good sized kitchen spoon of salt. Better salt the water to taste. Throw in a pound of Italian made spaghetti ... the Farina spaghetti. It requires a certain kind of wheat to make good macaroni. Boil for twenty minutes. Drain off water.

To the rich gravy you will find the roast swimming in add a small can of tomato paste, stirring in slowly. As this is poured over the spaghetti add grated Roman cheese. You will get it all properly dressed by using two forks, lifting and dropping the strands. Serve piping hot with an automatic revolver at hand so that the man who cuts his can be disposed of promptly. Some twine the spaghetti about the fork. Others just lead a mass of it to the face and bite off what they want at that particular mastication.

A good salad and Italian bread, to be secured at any small dealer's where the boss sings Santa Lucia in a thin high voice as he slices the salami, goes well with the roast. This layout will last an old bachelor or a deserted husband two or three days. It's grand when it's warmed up in a boiler.

93

# LXXII

## F. X. Leyendecker

## VEAU SAUTÉ MARENGO

During my Paris days (school days) I became very fond of two dishes and they still remain my favorites:

No. 1—Veau Sauté Marengo—nothing epicurean about this, but real tasty; a ragout of veal which must be served in a brown pot. It is flavored with tiny onions and mushrooms, olives and a delicious sauce. I have never found it quite so well prepared as in Paris.

Fry some small pieces of veal in oil, add one chopped onion, one head of crushed garlic and when it is well brown strain it, add one glass of white wine and reduce. Moisten it with one quart of brown sauce. Add two pounds fresh tomatoes and some fine herbs. Cook slowly for an hour and a half.

Put the meat in another pan, add few small onions cooked in butter, some small mushrooms already cooked.

Dress and serve on toast fried in butter.

No. 2—Vol au Vent Financière—a pastry form filled with mushrooms, cubes of chicken, something else, and a good sauce. This also seems not quite the same outside of Paris.

## VOL AU VENT FINANCIÉRE

Put four ounces of butter in a saucepan, add four ounces of cooked sweetbread cut in three-sixteenth inch squares, small bits of the white of chicken, some truffles, olives, mushrooms, kidney and cock's combs.

Moisten with one pint of Madeira sauce, let boil and despumate; when the sauce is done strain it through a tamis, fill your pastry crust and serve.

Editor's Note:—The recipes are French, and properly prepared and served, they will prove the real thing in Keokuk as well as in the Quartier Latin.

94

# LXXIII

## Eddie Cantor

## BOILED BEEF AND HORSERADISH SAUCE

I love boiled beef and horseradish sauce—I love it better than any other dish in the world!

Anybody knows how to boil beef. And a good horseradish sauce is made in this fashion.

Melt a good sized lump of the best butter—almost as big as an egg, is good sized. Add to this, first removing from the fire, about two tablespoonsful of flour. Stir the flour and butter together until the mixture is absolutely smooth, and then add cold milk—a trifle more than a half pint, a shade less than a pint. Put over a slow fire in a sauce pan or, for safety's sake, a double-boiler. Cook slowly until the sauce is of the desired consistency, and then add your horseradish. If you like the sauce very hot add a lot of horseradish. If you like it moderate, a little horseradish. The best way is to begin with a teaspoonful and keep adding and tasting until it's O. K. Salt and pepper to taste, of course. And, if you like it, a dash of celery salt.

# LXXIV

## Frazier Hunt

## STUFFED CELERY

I like food. I like almost any kind of food. I've eaten all varieties—in great cities and in out of the way corners of the world. And I've never found anything that I couldn't eat, if I were hungry enough!

But best of all I think that I like stuffed celery. It's easy to fix, and it's slightly out of the ordinary, and it's possible to consume a lot of it without being looked down upon by those who are dining with you. Because everybody eats a lot of stuffed celery.

To a half pound of Roquefort cheese add a quarter of a pound of butter. Cream them together until they are as smooth as it is possible to make any mixture containing Roquefort cheese. Then add a dessertspoonful—or a tablespoonful, if you like—of Worcestershire sauce. A little salt, and some paprika, enough to slightly color the mixture. And then—

Take stalks of celery—very white and crisp and fresh. And stuff the hollow side, until it bulges, with the Roquefort mixture. And serve with your dinner, or after dinner, or with the salad, or all alone. It doesn't matter when or where you place it on the menu, for it's apt to be the dominant note!

# LXXV

## William Slavins McNutt

## ORANGE COMPOTE

Orange Compote is my favorite dish. After my fourth I begin to forget that I'm a human being. After my sixth I can feel myself drifting into a blissfully comatose state—with only strength enough left to call for a seventh.

Orange Compote, at its best, may be obtained in any small Turkish or Armenian restaurant where the coffee is good and the dishes aren't too offensively clean. When made at home it is never quite the same—I don't know why. This, however, is the best working substitute that I am able to concoct.

Take as many oranges as your system is capable of absorbing, and peel them, removing all of the thin white inside skin, and all of the film-like tissue that divides an orange into sections. I forgot to mention that the orange should be large, luscious, juicy and free of seeds. Place the oranges in individual serving dishes and pour over them this sauce, while hot:

For about six oranges you will need one middle-sized jar of orange marmalade and one small can of Hawaiian pineapple. Put the marmalade, the pineapple—cut into small cubes—and the pineapple juice into a double boiler and cook, briskly, until the liquid begins to thicken. Then pour it over the uncooked oranges and allow them—each in its individual dish—to stand in the ice box until dessert time. Just before serving, sprinkle with a few pine nuts, or salted almonds. Pine nuts are best.

# LXXVI

## Stephen Vincent Benet

## ZITELLI'S MACARONI STEW

Take one-half pound of real Italian macaroni, boil it in plenty of water, slightly salted, till soft, say, about twenty minutes; take one quart of tomatoes, one-half pint of water and two ounces of fat bacon cut into small pieces. Now one onion and a small bunch of parsley; boil all these together (apart from the macaroni) for half an hour, then pass the mixture through a colander; add one tablespoonful of butter and season with salt and pepper to taste.

Put it on the fire again and let it boil for five minutes. Let the macaroni and the sauce both be very hot. In a tureen place a layer of the macaroni covered with grated cheese; then cover with a ladleful of the sauce and repeat the layers until the entire amount is served. It should be dished in deep soup plates for individual servings.

# LXXVII

## James R. Quirk

## TOMATO WIGGLE

To one pound of diced American cheese, add one can of Campbell's Tomato Soup. Heat over a slow fire until a thick, smooth mass has been obtained. And then—

Add one beaten egg, and follow it quickly with a cup of cream or very rich milk. Stir in a dessertspoonful of Worcestershire Sauce, and enough salt to give the proper kick.

Serve on soda crackers that have been heated—large soda crackers.

The name? That's just to make it difficult.

# LXXVIII

## Charles W. Eliot

## A FAVORITE MENU

I can hardly say that I have a "favorite dish." But a favorite menu for luncheon or dinner is clam soup, corned beef hash, and baked Indian pudding.

*Note.*—If you want to try Dr. Eliot's menu why not use Rex Beach's clam specialty?

Then for the corned beef hash get plenty of fine lean corned beef and cut it into one-eighth inch bits.

Chop one small onion into very fine particles. Take cold boiled potatoes (fairly firm) and cut or chop.

Prepare some drawn butter and add a few drops of Worcestershire sauce, salt and pepper. Now mix the meat, potatoes, onion and drawn butter. Mold and pat into small, flat, elliptical loaves (individual servings) and fry in a hot, lightly buttered pan. Turn frequently until well browned on both sides. Serve sprinkled with minced parsley.

Top off with this baked Indian pudding:

You must have 1 quart of milk, 3 eggs, ½ cup of the finest seeded raisins, 1 teaspoonful of salt, 2 heaping tablespoonsful of corn meal, 4 heaping tablespoonsful of sugar, 1 heaping tablespoonful of butter.

Boil the milk in a double boiler and sprinkle in the corn meal, stirring all the time. Cook twelve minutes.

Beat the eggs, adding the salt, sugar and a half teaspoonful of ground ginger. Add this mixture with the butter to milk and meal, then add the raisins and stir until perfectly mixed. Remove from the double boiler and bake for one hour.

You will agree with Dr. Eliot.

# LXXIX

## H. S. Cumming

## (Surgeon General, U.S.P.H.S.)

### VIRGINIA EGG BREAD

I am particularly fond of this dish—it is, I think, my favorite, and I pass along the recipe with the hope that others will find it as satisfying and delicious as do those who already list it among their favorites.

        1 cup water ground corn meal (white)
        2½ cups boiling water
        1 cup sweet milk
        3 or 4 eggs
        1 teaspoonful salt
        2 tablespoonsful butter
        2 teaspoonsful sugar

Stir boiling water into the sifted meal; add sweet milk; when cool break eggs into the mixture and beat thoroughly; add salt, sugar and butter melted. Bake in well buttered baking dish in hot oven.

# LXXX

## Joseph Santley

## COCOA CREAM CAKE

I will admit that it sounds a good deal like "pink sponge cake" to announce a preference for anything so epicureanly flippant as cocoa cream cake. But it is the one dish that I prefer above any other, and in justice to truth and accuracy, I repeat—my favorite is cocoa cream cake! And my own dear mother will have to stand the responsibility for whatever shame comes to me by openly declaring it. You see, she makes it. And it was from her I learned the secret of its concoction.

Here is the recipe:

Four eggs, one cup of sugar, one cup of cocoa, a teaspoonful of vanilla, and a teaspoonful of baking powder. Cream yolks of eggs and sugar well; add the vanilla. Sift the cocoa and baking powder well, and add to the eggs and sugar. Last of all stir in the whites of the eggs, beaten. Bake in two layers, for about ten minutes. When cold whip a pint of thick cream with a teaspoonful of vanilla and sugar to taste—placing half between the layers and half on top.
Oh, boy!

# LXXXI

## A. Hamilton Gibbs

## SQUAB EN CASSEROLE

In a casserole put generous layer of sliced onion sauté, two sliced tomatoes sauté, two cups of mushrooms, two cups of potato balls, and a little fresh parsley also sauté. (All the vegetables should be fried in butter). On top place, breast up, a squab or a one-pound chicken—one for each person. On each breast place a slice of crisp fried bacon. Over all pour some rich well-seasoned brown sauce, filling the casserole up with the chicken breasts—three-quarters full—preferably with a cup of sherry added last, if your cellar will still produce it!

Place the casserole in a hot oven, uncovered. When the breasts are brown, cool oven to a moderate heat, cover the casserole and cook for two hours. Then remove the casserole and serve from dish.

The result is an epicurean masterpiece.

# LXXXII

## Richard Barthelmess

## SPICED GRAPES

This dish is always reminiscent, to me, of low New England farmhouses, with green blinds. You know the kind—set far back from the road, among tall trees, with hollyhocks, and rose geraniums and old fashioned pinks in the garden. When I see such a house—and I can, sometimes, by closing my eyes—I can always smell the pungent scent of spiced grapes, cooking away on an immaculate kitchen range.

This is the rule for making spiced grapes. A rule that most New England families seem to follow.

To seven pounds of grapes there should be added these materials—three pounds of granulated sugar, one cup of vinegar, two tablespoonsful of ground cinnamon, and one tablespoonful of ground cloves.

Weigh the grapes, wash and pulp them. Cook the pulp until the seeds are loosened—then press the mass through a sieve. Cook the skins just as long as you cook the pulps. Put them on the same stove, but in separate kettles. Add the strained pulps to the skins, then vinegar, sugar, and spices. And cook until the mixture thickens.

This, when served with cold meat, changes a commonplace supper of left-overs into a feast.

# LXXXIII

## Don Juan y Gayangos

### (Ambassador to the United States, from Spain)

### EGG PLANT AU GRATIN

Peel the egg plant.
Whiten it in salty water, and dry.
Fry, in butter, with salt sprinkled on each piece.
Place in a dish with grated cheese, tomato sauce, and mushrooms, which have been cut into small pieces and put thickly between the layers of egg plant.
Bake, until well cooked, in a moderate oven.

# LXXXIV

## Samuel G. Blythe

## TRIPE Á LA MODE DE CAEN Á LA ROY CARRUTHERS

Only an artist should attempt to make Tripe à la Mode de Caen because only an artist can make it. It requires the soul of a poet, the spirit of a painter, and the exaltation of a violin virtuoso in the maker as a prerequisite for its concoction. Of course, it may be eaten by the commonalty, but it is too good for them. It really is a dish for the intelligentsia.

There are not more than a dozen people in the United States who have the temperament and the touch required. One of these is Roy Carruthers. And herewith, as my favorite recipe, I set down the complicated but necessary, procedure for producing this work of art:

Take four pounds of fresh honeycomb tripe and one pound of fresh manyplies tripe (the thickest part) and wash thoroughly in many changes of fresh water. Drain well, and scrape to have all absolutely clean. Take two calf's feet and carefully bone each foot and cut into pieces two inches square. Have a large earthen pot, scrupulously clean, and line sides and bottom of this pot with very thin slices of larding pork. Place tripe and cut up feet in pot.

Add two small red carrots, two white onions with two cloves stuck in each, and half of a sound, seeded pepper. Make a bouquet of two leeks, two branches of celery, three branches of parsley, and a sprig of thyme, marjoram, a blade of mace and a bay leaf—only one. Put this bouquet in the pot and pour in a half pint of white wine, a pint of cider and a quart of consomme or white broth. Season with a full teaspoon of salt and half a spoon of black pepper.

Now make a stiff dough with a pound of white flour and two gills of water, roll out on a table until you have enough to cover the pot, and cover closely, making sure there can be no evaporation.

Place pot in a very slow oven and cook for fifteen hours.

Then lift up the cover, skim off the fat, and remove the bouquet of herbs and the vegetables.

Chop together six shallots, or scallions if shallots are not procurable, the red part of a carrot, a bean of sound garlic, two ounces of raw ham and an ounce of raw lean pork. Place this hash in

106

a saucepan with a tablespoon of melted butter, cook gently on the fire for five minutes, stirring lightly, and then pour in half a gill of cognac and let it reduce briskly until it is nearly dry.

Put the contents of the pot on the saucepan, add a gill of pure tomato juice, mix lightly with a wooden spoon, and cook slowly for forty-five minutes.

Then dress the tripe on a deep hot dish, sprinkle a little freshly chopped parsley over and send to table very hot with twelve slices of toasted French bread.

That is real Tripe à la mode de Caen. All others are imitations.

# LXXXV

## Charles H. Taylor

## CLAM CHOWDER

Try out salt pork. Take out the scraps. Cut up onions and fry them in the pork fat until they are a golden brown. Open clams and save all the clam water. (Most chefs steam the clams first because they are so much easier to handle, but if you want the real flavor you want to shell the clams, wash the meat over carefully and let the clam water settle and dip it out instead of pouring it into your kettle so as to leave out the sand.)

Add to the onions enough hot water to cover them, put in clam water and the bellies of the clams. Cook until the bellies of the clams have practically disappeared (about two hours). Then add whatever more hot water is necessary, add the rest of your clam meat, after having first cut off the black end of the head, and run the meat through the coarsest cutting disk of your meat grinder. Cook until clams are very nearly done and then add your sliced white potato. Cook again until the potatoes are done. Then add whatever milk you put in and let it come to a boil. Put into the chowder what we call Boston cracker. They are shaped like a water cracker only they are soft. Split them in halves. These will soften up immediately and you can then serve your chowder.

Do not use any flour for thickening. If the chowder is prepared and the bellies of the clams cooked as above, this will make the broth thicken up.

# LXXXVI

## Cyrus H. K. Curtis

## BAKED BEANS

*(My Favorite Dish)*

To prepare Mr. Curtis' favorite food is no difficult task and any number of methods original and otherwise may be followed.

For the best results have a large covered bean pot and the rest is easy.

Select fine white or navy beans. Wash them thoroughly and let them soak in clear water for several hours—most folks soak them all night.

Place the beans in the pot with several pieces of salt pork (with fat), cover with water slightly salted. Put the lid on the pot and bake in a moderate oven until done. That's plain baked beans.

Chili sauce or tomato catsup or chopped tomatoes may be added to taste.

Look at the beans occasionally and add water if they seem too dry or in danger of burning.

Another method which produces wonderful results is to omit the pork and tomato preparations and add generous lumps of butter and brown sugar—better still, add genuine sorghum molasses. When you do it this way be extra careful to see that just enough water is added in small quantities to prevent burning.

Always remove from the oven while the beans are still whole. If baked too long they will break up. The time necessary for baking will vary according to the heat of the oven and the length of time the beans were soaked.

# LXXXVII

## Frederick Arnold Kummer

## SPAGHETTI DIABOLIQUE

Brown one and a half pounds top plate of beef in half a cup of boiling olive oil for one hour, turning frequently. Mince the shells of four sweet peppers, one bunch of celery, one bunch of parsley, three large onions, two sections of clove garlic, add a salt-spoonful of ground thyme, a teaspoonful of salt, one of black pepper and red pepper to taste. Add one quart of tomatoes, pour over the beef, cook for an hour, add a pint of water and cook slowly for two hours more.

To make the spaghetti: Measure a quart of flour, break in yolks of three eggs, add three half eggshells full of ice water, work to the proper consistency, roll and cut into thin strips. When dry cook in boiling salted water for twenty minutes.

Place spaghetti in the center of a dish, pour the sauce and shredded meat around it, and serve.

*Editor's Note:*—From the several "favorite dishes" of spaghetti mentioned in this volume it would seem that there is a decided male preference for this particular article of diet. Mr. Kummer goes the limit and tells how to make the spaghetti, itself!

# LXXXVIII

## Albert D. Lasker

## CHICKEN PAPRIKA

Say a five pound chicken—do it this way and see how you like it.

Slice four small onions. Put one-sixth pound of butter into pan, add onions and let cook over fire until soft and a light brown in color. Add two teaspoonsful of paprika and put in the chicken piece by piece, fitting into kettle; add 1¼ tablespoonsful of salt, cover tightly and cook until soft (two hours or more). Remove the chicken, and into the gravy add 1¼ tablespoonsful of canned tomatoes; shake in a tablespoonful of flour and stir well; add ¾ pint of sour cream and stir well over the fire. Strain over the chicken; heat again and serve.

# LXXXIX

## Henry van Dyke

## FISH CHOWDER

I will say that I like to cook (and if I have good luck, to eat) a dish for which the following is the recipe:

First catch your fish with hook and line,—salmon, trout or bass, cod, haddock or blue-fish. Then obtain a good sized kettle and put into it, first a layer of sliced potatoes, then a fine sprinkling of fine sliced onion, then a layer of fat pork cut into small cubes, then a layer of fish, skinned and sliced, then a layer of crackers or thin pilot biscuit. Sprinkle salt and pepper on each layer according to taste. Repeat the layers from three to five times according to the size of your kettle. Fill the pot moderately full with water and put it on the fire to cook slowly. If the water gets low replenish it. You can tell when the dish is done by testing the potatoes or the fish with a fork. As a rule it should take about an hour to cook. Just before the end put in two or three cupfuls of milk. If your taste is slightly vitiated by contact with the world you may add a double spoonful of some spicy sauce. But for my part I like a chowder best au naturel.

# XC

## Macklyn Arbuckle

## SOUTHERN GUMBO Á LA "COUNTY CHAIRMAN"

A year-old fowl. Joint it as you would for frying.

Soup kettle ready on the back of the stove with cold water.

Then, the frying pan—

About one-half dozen thin slices of the best bacon. Reserve this for the kettle later.

Bacon fat in the frying pan—fry the chicken very brown. As soon as each piece of chicken is brown place it in the kettle—then put the kettle over the fire. Let it boil.

Add six small onions or three large ones. Sliced and fried in the bacon grease.

Onions fried golden brown.

Then to the onions add a can of tomatoes or the equivalent of sliced tomatoes.

Keep stirring from the bottom to prevent burning.

All must cook until it has thickened.

While cooking add chili peppers cut fine, green peppers the same, also okra.

Add one or two large bay leaves and season to taste with salt and pepper.

Onions, tomatoes and peppers should be added to the chicken in the kettle when they have cooked sufficiently.

If fresh okra is not available use the best canned kind.

About ten minutes before the Gumbo is ready add—

One can of Golden Bantam Corn.

To serve with the Gumbo have a dish of perfectly cooked rice. You may use the same general formula for Crab or Oyster Gumbo. A Combination Salad is about the only thing worth serving with Gumbo. Although you might wash it down with a bottle of PRE-WAR IMPORTED CLARET—HELP!!!!

# XCI

## John Taintor Foote

## MORELS SAUTÉ

There is a dish—a gastronomical ecstasy—the faintest conception of which is magnificently beyond the pen. The fork is the one utensil that can convey to the uninitiated the unique, the utterly sublime flavor of Morels sauté.

A Morel is—in the vernacular of the countryside—a sponge mushroom. It is to be found in ancient, unplowed orchards during the pastel phase of spring when apple trees blossom and bees zoom and bumble and hum in a languid shower of pink and white petals.

Close to a girthy apple tree, scabrous with age, pock-marked by the bills of countless woodpeckers, the Morels, now and then— alas, it is only now and then—poke up through the cold, damp, chocolate-colored earth and flourish shyly for a fortnight or so.

A full day's tramping through orchard after orchard may win perhaps two dozen of these tiny sponges that have absorbed the very essence of spring. They are almost the exact color of the matted, winter-killed grass in which they nestle to defy all but the most careful searching. A full day's work for each two dozen, but never was a day's wage more ample, more exquisitely satisfying.

Take the hard-won double dozen home. Give them in reverent silence to the cook. She knows—if, by the grace of God, she was with you so long ago as the previous spring—just what to do. She will plop the Morels into well salted water, there to remain the night through. In the morning she will place them in a colander to drain for half an hour. She will then transfer them to a frying pan of hot butter, where they will sputter and sizzle for twenty minutes. During that twenty minutes there will waft into the living room, where you are making a pitiful pretense of reading the morning paper, an odor straight from the kitchens of heaven.

You throw down the newspaper and burst with glaring eyes into the dining room. You seat yourself at the table and fiddle wildly with knife and fork and spoon.... Years later the waitress appears with a dish and then—I faint—I swoon—I cannot go on!

114

# XCII

## Maurice Francis Egan

## A DIPLOMATIST'S RECEIPT FOR WELSH RABBIT

I have no hesitation in saying that my recipe for Welsh Rabbit is the best yet invented. It has an international reputation. It has been eaten with gusto by Russians, Turks and some Englishmen who, strange to say, are distinguished gourmets. There have been Frenchmen who were too reserved, perhaps, in their praise of it, but then it must be remembered that Welsh rabbit is not sympathetic with the Gallic temperament. The French prefer timbales de fromage.

Put a large chafing dish over the hot water pan in which the water must be boiling. Never let the temperature of the heat change for a moment; therefore a big alcohol lamp is preferable. Grate ordinary cheese or cut it into the shape of dice. Drop in a lump of butter of the size of an English walnut. Pour into the pan a pint of near beer or near Budweiser. Slightly heat it. In the old days musty ale was everything. To-day the symbol of beer is almost sufficient. Drop in a half teaspoonful of strong red pepper and then a tablespoonful of paprika,—paprika being merely a flavor and not a condiment. Keep the beer hot; then drop two tablespoons of Worcestershire sauce, a tablespoon of catsup and a half teaspoon of mustard. When this mixture boils, put in the cheese and stir in one direction until the mixture assumes the consistency of cream.

Use the thick plates sold in the department stores especially for Welsh Rabbit. Have them heated so that the cheese will sizzle when it touches them. Have ready a sufficient number of pieces of toasted bread, the crust carefully cut off. When the cheese is sufficiently plastic, dip a round of toast into it, let it remain for a second, transfer it to the hot plate and at once ladle the mixture in the pan over the toast with neatness and dispatch and you will have an unprecedented success, if no conversation is permitted until the rabbit is eaten. The sound of a human voice lowers its temperature. Coffee or tea must never be partaken of until the morsels are disposed of. During the eating process, Budweiser is a substitute for the real thing—which was musty ale or the Dog's Head variety.

# XCIII

## Livingston Farrand

## SAUSAGE AND GRIDDLE CAKES

I think I would say that my favorite dish is sausage and griddle cakes for breakfast on a cold winter morning. I would call attention to the fact that the sausages should be in cake form and not in skins and that the griddle cakes should be of wheat flour. I am sure there are millions of Americans who agree with me.

*Editor's Note:*—Here is the best of a dozen tried recipes for the cakes.

To one cup of Hecker's, or any excellent self-raising flour (not pancake!) add a full half cup of milk and a beaten egg mixed together. A little cream will help at this point, but it isn't absolutely necessary.

Melt, now, a lump of butter the size of a good big walnut and stir it into the mixture. Beat for a moment and if the consistency does not seem just right add a shade more of milk or flour. The mixture or batter should be about as thick as molasses in the winter time.

For the very perfection in results bake the cakes on a soapstone griddle and serve with the best maple syrup obtainable.

This recipe can be safely doubled any number of times and then some! As above it serves two unless more are desired, in which case it is easy to duplicate in no time.

# XCIV

## F. Ziegfeld, Jr.

## LITTLE CHICKEN TARTS

Here is a dish that I am very fond of and it is really very easy to prepare. The tart molds may be purchased already made, which simplifies things somewhat if you do not want to bother with the dough, but in case you cannot get them here is the whole process and I can vouch for the results.

2 cups of chopped chicken (cooked) or one large can Chicken à la King
½ cup evaporated milk
2 eggs
1 onion
2 cups sifted flour
½ cup shortening
½ cup water
1 teaspoonful salt
Pepper
Parsley
Ice water

Mix salt and flour—cut in the chilled shortening with two knives until the mixture is as fine as meal. With a broad-bladed knife stir in ice water slowly until dough clings around knife in a ball, leaving sides of bowl perfectly clean. Toss dough on floured bread board. Flour the rolling pin and roll it out very thin. Keep the pin well floured. Rub the outside of patty pans or jelly molds with a little shortening and lay dough over these smoothly, bringing it well over the edge. Bake upside down for about ten minutes in a hot oven. If Chicken à la King is used for a filling it will not require any special preparation, but if you really want to cook, and you use the cold chicken, proceed as follows:

Cut the chicken in small pieces, but do not mince. Mince onion and cook until slightly brown in a little butter. Stir in a tablespoonful of flour, add milk and water. When smooth add chicken and season to taste. When bubbling take from the fire and stir in the slightly beaten eggs. Let cool, then fill the pastry shells.

117

The remainder of the pastry dough should have been kept in the ice box. Get it out. Roll it thin as before. Cut in round pieces to cover the tops of the tarts. Wet the edges of the tarts with cold water; press on the covers, bringing the edges well down as they shrink a bit in baking. Slit the tops before putting on. Press the edges with tines of fork. Garnish with parsley.

# XCV

## Harold Lloyd

## LEMON LAYER CAKE

This, when properly gummy, is as good for a comedian to throw as a custard pie. Only it's too good for that sort of treatment—which sounds rather like an Irish bull!

The layer cake doesn't interest me especially. After all, it's only an excuse for the frosting. Any sort of layer cake recipe will answer—and, according to the best cook I know, my grandmother—there are a hundred such recipes. It's the filling that I find important. Here is the rule, and it sounds too simple to be true!

Take one beaten egg, one cup of sugar, the juice and grated rind of one lemon. Mix them all together, hit or miss, and place them in a double boiler over a hot fire. Cook until the mixture begins to get very thick, stirring constantly. Then take from the stove and beat until the whole assumes a creamy texture. Spread between the layers of any cake. This recipe makes enough filling for two thin layers, or one thick one—which I prefer. It can be doubled, tripled, and so on—ad infinitum—depending entirely upon the number of layers in the cake.

*Editor's Note:*—This is a good, and unusual, recipe for layer cake. To two eggs, well beaten, add gradually one cup of granulated sugar. To one cup of unsifted flour add one teaspoonful cream of tartar and one half teaspoonful of soda. Sift. Then add one half cup of boiling milk with one teaspoonful of melted butter in it, and one teaspoonful of vanilla. The mixture will be almost like batter, and should be baked in two layers.

# XCVI

## Luther Burbank

## TURKEY Á LA BURBANK

*"The best ever."*[1]

For an ordinary ten-pound turkey steam 2½ hours or until the muscles of the leg can be readily pierced with a dining fork. Take steamer from the fire and carefully remove the turkey to the roasting pan.

Meantime, prepare the dressing as follows: One loaf of bread, ordinary baker's size, or same amount of other bread, slice and toast slowly but thoroughly to a light golden color; while hot, spread butter on each slice just as a hungry boy would like it. Place in a deep dish. The cooked giblets, which, with the juice of one lemon and three whole large onions, should be ground all together in a meat grinder with

1 teaspoon salt
½ teaspoon cayenne pepper
1 teaspoon powdered sage
2 teaspoon summer savory
2 tablespoons sugar

These should be well sifted and then added to the ground vegetables and giblets, and with the meat juice saved from steaming, thoroughly mixed with the bread and all cut and mashed to about the consistency of thick mush. After filling, the turkey should be placed in an oven not too hot, and slowly roasted an hour or more.

Prepared as above, little or no basting will be necessary, but a few thin slices of bacon laid over the fowl will add flavor. Add no oysters, eggs, chestnuts or other abominations.

---

[1] Mr. Burbank says so himself. If he said he could make turkey look and taste like brook trout, he probably could.

# XCVII

## Raymond McKee

## TO COOK RABBITS

I do not profess to be a cook of the first rank, or even the fourth or ninth; but when it comes to cooking rabbits I'll put on the kitchen apron with any cook, amateur or professional, in the country—(managers, please note!). And I'll abide by the decision of any judge of rabbit flesh.

Out in California, where I live most of the time on my mountain yacht, you can get a lot of rabbits by shooting them—if you are good. But it's easier to buy them, and they taste the same.

To cook a rabbit right do it this way: First—get the rabbit, clean and cut into six pieces. Soak the pieces in salt water for several hours—I usually soak 'em all night and right up to the time for cooking. This whitens and improves the meat.

When you are ready to cook, dry the pieces; roll them in a beaten egg and then in cracker crumbs. Put the pieces into a very hot pan with plenty of butter and fry it to a golden brown. When the color is right put water into the pan so that the rabbit is about half covered. Cover the pan with a tight lid and steam slowly until the water is all gone. Then serve.

Now, if you can substitute an ordinary claret for the salt water mentioned first, and if you have more claret in which to steam the fried rabbit you may know the perfect dish!

# XCVIII

## Will Deming

I can vouch for all of these:

## VIRGINIA HAM

Cover an eight-pound ham with cold water. Add a pint of cider vinegar; one-half pound of brown sugar; six sticks of cinnamon and a heaping tablespoonful of cloves. Let this boil for four hours. Push back on the stove and let it stay all night. In the morning skin it and put it in a hot oven for half an hour.

## LEMON PIE

The filling: In a cup full of sugar mix thoroughly a heaping tablespoonful and one-half of flour. Grate the skin of one lemon, and add the juice. Then add the yolks of two eggs and a cup of water, also a pinch of salt. Stir this thoroughly, all together. Put into a double boiler and let it cook until it is thick and smooth. Then pour it into the cooked pie crust. Add a teaspoonful of water to the whites of the eggs, and a pinch of salt. Then beat until stiff. Cover your pie with this mixture and then sprinkle granulated sugar on top of the meringue. Don't mix the sugar and the meringue. Put under the broiler to brown.

The crust: Mix two good sized tablespoonfuls of lard with one and a half cups of flour. Mix this with your fingers thoroughly, until it feels like corn meal, although much larger. Add ice water until the mixture holds together; then roll on a floured board. In baking the crust for a lemon pie, either puncture the crust all over with a fork or bake it on the outside of your pie tin. This will keep the crust from creeping.

# A DRESSING

(For stuffed tomatoes, cold meat or potato salad.)

Melt a large tablespoonful of butter. Add a saucer of vinegar to the yolks of two eggs. Then add a teaspoonful of dry mustard and a teaspoonful of sugar. Stir the mixture—sugar and eggs—into the vinegar; then add it to the butter which you have on the stove, melting. Keep stirring this until it gets thick, and remember that it will be much thicker when it is cold. In case you wish to use this for potato salad, don't make it very thick.

# XCIX

## Charles W. Chessar

## ("Beefsteak Charlie")

## TIPS ON STEAK

"Why can't we have steaks like this one when we dine at home?" Thousands of people have asked me that question during the eight years that have given a real significance to the sobriquet, "Beefsteak Charlie."

And my honest answer to that question has always been: "You can't—unless your butcher is willing to hang your beef for four or five weeks—and then you probably would not want to buy it because of its appearance."

Many people ask me how to cook a steak. There is really no secret about the way it should be done—but most home cooks put the steak into a cold broiler and light the fire. That is fatal! And it is just as fatal if the fire has only been burning a few minutes. The broiler should burn full tilt for some time—until it is blazing hot. Then introduce your steak and let the intense heat of the broiler seal it instantly. If there is a secret, that's it!

But keep this in mind: the most careful broiling will not help if the beef is too fresh. Fresh beef simply will not do if you want the real thing. Buy the choicest cuts of sirloin or porterhouse from beef that has been hung at least four weeks; broil in the way I have described and your dinner guests will register many polite hints for another invitation. I might add that if the beef is right you will not have to worry about a sauce. Butter, salt, and pepper will properly dress the finest steak in the world.

# C

## Arthur T. Vance

## SALADE Á LA TURC

I don't profess to shine much as a cook. I would rather have somebody do it for me, but there are one or two things that I sometimes like to fix on my own hook.

Years ago there was some sort of a Centennial Exposition out in Nashville, Tenn. I don't remember what they had to celebrate, but at any rate I had to take it in. I didn't know a soul and good old Al Williams, the snake man—who died last year—gave me a letter of introduction to the Turk who ran the Hoochy-Koochy show on the midway. It is the only time I ever used a letter of introduction with efficiency and delectation. This Turk—who, incidentally, was one of the finest looking chaps I ever saw, and a man of education—welcomed me with open arms. First of all I had to see the show, and I was so enthusiastic about the gyrations of the sumptuous beauties that he did me the great honor of asking me to dine with him, en famille. It was a great experience. All the Hoochy-koochy dancers were there, in their stage costumes, with ma and pa and mother-in-law, and mother's great uncle and a rabble of other folks, large and small. We had a lot of funny things to eat, but there was one dish that really appealed to me. They called it "Salada" and I ate of it in such copious portions that my friend, the Turk, insisted on showing me how it was made. I have made it many times since for my own pleasure, at least—and most folk who try it once will try it again.

It is a salad of ripe tomatoes, cucumbers and onions. The main point is that you must not slice them up but—after you peel your onions, cucumbers and tomatoes—put them whole into a chopping bowl, and chop them into chunks with a chopping knife. The chunks should be about as large as the end of your thumb. After the chopping operation, put the whole business on the ice until it gets good and cold. Then drain off the juice.

Add a sharp French dressing, get a big spoon and a plate and go to it. If it doesn't taste good, I'll eat it myself.

# PANDORA FRENCH DRESSING

I have discovered that the secret of French dressing, to my way of thinking, is to use plenty of salt. When I make it at home—say for five or six people—I take an ordinary salt dish or saucer and cover the bottom with a lot of salt. Add black pepper and some of that Chili powder that comes from a place down in Texas. This Chili powder has a better flavor than paprika, and has a sort of onion taste to it, but don't use too much of it. Then I cover this with a good quantity of olive oil and beat it up with a fork until it gets stiff. It is a good idea to have the olive oil cold. Then add your vinegar—good, old-fashioned cider vinegar. There is a lot of it around nowadays because, while it is easy to turn sweet cider into hard, it is a good deal easier to turn hard cider into vinegar. You add the vinegar to suit your taste—and this depends a good deal on the kind of salad you are going to have. For asparagus I like the dressing a little tart. For lettuce, not so tart. But this is a matter you can easily adjust to your own satisfaction.

# WELSH RABBIT Á LA MORGAN ROBERTSON

I wonder how many folk who read these pages remember Morgan Robertson. Poor old Morgan is dead and gone, now, but in his day he wrote some of the best sea stories ever put into English. He used to keep bachelor hall in a funny little studio down on 25th Street, off Sixth Avenue, New York—and when his friends came to call his special delight was a Welsh Rabbit. He told me how to make it, and I am trying to pass the recipe on. The beauty of Robertson's rabbit was that it never got stringy.

First you put a good-sized lump of butter into a chafing dish and let it sizzle. Add some Coleman's mustard and paprika and stir it round a bit. For six people I would use two pounds of cheese. Real old New York State full cream cheese—none of this odoriferous imported stuff. The kind of cheese they used to make down on the farm. Cut it up in chunks and put it in the pan with a little beer (near beer will do), or you could use milk. Keep adding a little more beer as the cheese commences to melt and put in a little Worcestershire sauce, if you like it. When it is well melted take a heaping tablespoonful of corn starch, mix it with a little water, and mix it with the mess. Meanwhile keep stirring it. Let it bubble and when it comes to the consistency of pancake batter (meanwhile keep stirring it—you can't stir it too much!) it is ready to serve. And please serve it on toasted bread. If there is anything makes me tired, it is to have Welsh Rabbit served on crackers—it isn't the same thing. Don't be afraid the rabbit will get stringy, because it won't. Some folks put the corn starch in dry, instead of mixing it with water. Either way is right. Season it to suit yourself. But for the love of Mike don't beat an egg up in it. That's another kind of fish entirely.

# CI

## Baron de Cartier

### (Ambassador to the United States from Belgium)

## WATERZOIE DE VOLAILLE

Without doubt the most popular national dish of Belgium is Waterzoie de Volaille—a most delectable and satisfying soup of chicken. In Brussels the dish reaches perfection under the magic of the chef of the famous restaurant the "Filet de Sole," known to amateurs of good cooking in almost every country of Europe.

I am going to tell you how they do it at the "Filet de Sole." First of course you will secure a fine young fowl—chicken—and, after it has been perfectly cleaned and dressed, you will rub it well with a piece of lemon. Now cut it up as you would for frying.

Next prepare the casserole or vessel in which the soup will be made by generously buttering the sides and bottom. Over the bottom of the vessel place a bed of fine julienne composed of one third of fine white celery (remove all fibers or "strings") one-third of the white part of leek and one-third of white onion. To this add a bouquet composed of a half leaf of laurel, a soupçon of thyme enclosed in a few roots of parsley, the roots having been well scraped and washed.

Upon this bed place the pieces of chicken and over the whole pour a little more than a quart of dry white wine and veal broth— one third broth and two thirds wine. Water may be used instead of the broth but the latter is preferable. Season with kitchen salt, freshly ground white pepper and a pinch of clove.

Bring the mixture to the boiling point and allow it to simmer and steam under a tight cover for at least thirty-five minutes.

Take out the bouquet and pass the roots through a metal strainer. The extract is to be added to the soup. Now add a large pinch of bread crumbs.

At this point you will turn the soup into a large tureen and quickly add the rapidly beaten yolks of four eggs, two wine glasses of extra thick cream and a few thimblefuls of fine butter.

Complete the liaison by adding the pieces of chicken and, with a final sprinkle of chopped parsley, the Waterzoie is ready for the table and for your delectation.

128

# CII

## Dean Cornwell

## SPAGHETTI-MY-STYLE

After thinking over all of the dishes that I like—searching for the favorite—I come right back to the old standby, Spaghetti, and am forced to admit that it is my favorite.

You know how to cook the spaghetti itself, I'm sure, so I will just tell you how to make the sauce that I concocted some years ago and you'll like it.

Get a big iron kettle and put into it a lot of fine beef cut into small squares, some chopped bacon, dried mushrooms (the kind you get at any little Italian store) a can of tomatoes and some sliced onions. The dried mushrooms should be soaked for an hour or two before cooking.

Cover the materials with plenty of water and season with salt, brown sugar, and Mexican chili powder. Cook slowly all day—the longer the better, I find.

When you are simply famished and cannot wait any longer, ladle the sauce onto the steaming hot spaghetti and enjoy a real meal. The sauce is still better, in my opinion, when warmed up the second day.

9 798888 302897